Keeping Heads Above Water

Keeping Heads Above Water examines the settlement of Salvadorean refugees in Costa Rica. It focuses on urban employment programs designed to make them self-sufficient. These programs were funded and implemented by various international and domestic, governmental and nongovernmental agencies. The book addresses the question of why some small urban refugee enterprises failed, and how and why others survive and succeeded. This analysis is placed in the framework of theories that deal with the survival of petty commodity production in the capitalist economy. The unique contribution of this book is that it relates refugee settlement to theories of comparative development.

Two theoretical explanations are presented in the book. According to the first, small noncapitalist enterprises are viable as long as they avoid competition with capitalist firms. According to the second, known as the articulation approach, petty commodity producers are functional to capital accumulation in the capitalist sector and are therefore constantly reproduced by it. The book criticizes both of these approaches for placing too much emphasis on external aspects of production. Instead, it suggests that internal aspects of production, such as technology, labour relations, and organization of production, need to be examined in order to understand how informal petty commodity producers survive the competition with capitalist enterprises.

TANYA BASOK is an assistant professor in the Department of Anthropology and Sociology, University of Windsor.

Keeping Heads Above Water

Salvadorean Refugees in Costa Rica

TANYA BASOK

McGill-Queen's University Press
Montreal & Kingston • London • Buffalo

© McGill-Queen's University Press 1993
ISBN 0-7735-0977-1

Legal deposit second quarter 1993
Bibliothèque nationale du Québec

Printed in Canada on acid-free paper

This book has been published with the help of a grant
from the Social Science Federation of Canada, using
funds provided by the Social Sciences and Humanities
Research Council of Canada, and with the aid of a
grant from the Office of the Dean, Faculty of Social
Science, University of Windsor.

Canadian Cataloguing in Publication Data

Basok, Tanya, 1958–
    Keeping heads above water: Salvadorean refugees in
    Costa Rica
    Includes bibliographical references and index.
    ISBN 0-7735-0977-1
    1. Salvadorans – Costa Rica – Social conditions.
    2. Salvadorans – Costa Rica – Economic conditions.
    3. Refugees, Political – El Salvador. 4. Refugees,
    Political – Costa Rica. I. Title.
    JV7413.B38 1993   325'.21'097284097286   C92-090715-6

Typeset in Times 11/13 by
Caractéra production graphique inc., Quebec City.

Contents

Tables

Preface

The refugee phenomenon is not new: for centuries people have been forced to flee as a result of wars, feuds, raids, famines, and persecution of individuals. What distinguishes the current refugee crisis is its unprecedented scale.

Factors that led to the recent refugee explosion can be traced to the colonial expansion that retarded economic growth in many Third World countries and created great disparities in wealth, not only between the developed and developing countries but inside developing countries as well. These disparities in wealth continued to grow even after developing countries reached formal independence. National elites, subservient to foreign interests, need a system of repression for those who dare to challenge the status quo. To protect their own economic interests, foreign countries send military aid, advisers, and, at times, troops to repress dissent. Economic underdevelopment, dependence, and political repression go hand in hand. In spite of repression, however, popular discontent in some countries erupted into liberation struggles and revolutions attacking old foundations (in Angola, Mozambique, Vietnam, Nicaragua, El Salvador, Namibia, Guatemala, and Cuba). These struggles brought about direct and indirect foreign interventions (the United States in El Salvador and Chile, for example, the USSR in Afghanistan, and South

Africa in Mozambique). Both repression of dissidents and revolutionary struggles resulted in masses of people fleeing the areas of conflict.

Furthermore, the very process of decolonization has created massive refugee movements. Decolonization in Asia and Africa led to the creation of ethnically heterogeneous states where access to power is limited to members of particular ethnic groups. Ethnic clashes (at times culminating in separatist movements) result in considerable violence in these new states. Members of entire ethnic groups become uprooted and seek protection in neighbouring states (Zolberg, Suhrke, and Aguayo 1989).

Symptoms of political and economic imbalance that have been fermenting since the end of the fifteenth century in Third World countries have come to the surface and revealed themselves in violent confrontations. It is estimated that since the late 1940s at least forty million refugees have been uprooted as a result of political and ethnic conflicts in developing countries (Zolberg, Suhrke, and Aguayo 1989, 229).

The crisis began escalating in the early 1960s, provoked by liberation struggles in Algeria, Zaire, and Rwanda, and by armed confrontations between the north and the south in Sudan. At the same time, Asian countries (China, Bangladesh, and India) were also undergoing political turmoil, creating masses of refugees. The global refugee crisis escalated even further in the mid 1970s. Africa and Asia continued to generate massive flows of uprooted people. In addition, military repression in South American countries (Chile, Uruguay, Argentina, Brazil, and others) contributed to the growth of people in need of protection. The refugee crisis exploded, with ethnic confrontations in Sri Lanka and Lebanon, revolutionary conflicts in Central America, Mozambique, and Afghanistan, and violence in Sudan, Chad, and Uganda (Zolberg, Surhke, and Aguayo 1989, 227–9). The collapse of the Soviet empire has brought simmering ethnic resentments to a boil, at times resulting in violent ethnic clashes. Separatist struggles in Yugoslavia have also caused significant bloodshed. Thousands of refugees escaping ethnic violence in this region are likely to pour over the borders to neighbouring countries.

The scale of the movement is not the only characteristic distinguishing the current refugee crisis. In the past, victims of economic and political conflicts were able to obtain asylum in neighbouring countries. Recently, however, such a free population movement is blocked by entry and exit rules (Weiner 1985). In addition to being viewed as a violation of sovereignty, refugee masses create a drain on local resources. There is growing concern among most developing states to limit flows of uninvited people by tougher immigration laws that prevent the possibility of permanent asylum.

At the same time, developed countries are even more reluctant to shelter refugees. They are prepared to resettle only a small fraction of them. In the mid and late 1980s, Canada and Australia, for instance, each accepted about 12,000 refugees annually from the country of first asylum. The United States, with a population ten times that of Canada, accepted 70,000 refugees per year. In Europe, only Sweden and Norway had quotas of more than 1000 refugees a year (*Toronto Star*, 8 March 1987).

Since very few refugees are selected for resettlement, many choose to claim refugee status while already in the developing country. In 1983 some 72,000 non-European refugees requested asylum in Western Europe. In 1984 the figure increased to 102,000. In the same period, over 21,000 formal asylum applications were submitted in the United States and 20,000 in Canada (ICIHI 1986, 34–5).

This road to permanent resettlement is wrought with numerous difficulties and dangers. Some developed country governments prevent asylum seekers from setting foot in their country. According to the Independent Commission on International Humanitarian Issues, the United States has intercepted boat loads of Haitians and sent them back home. In 1985 the British government imposed visa restrictions on all Sri Lankans in order to prevent the arrival of Tamil asylum seekers. Some asylum applicants are denied a full hearing of their case. A number of European governments allow border guards and local police to reject asylum seekers. In the United States, the immigration authorities have been pressing many new arrivals to accept voluntary departure, thereby waiving their right to an asylum hearing. In 1981 more than 10,000 out of 13,000 Salvadoreans were stopped at the Mexican border (ICIHI 1986, 39). With respect to the human rights of asylum seekers, the Independent Commission on International Humanitarian Issues writes:

Once inside the country, asylum seekers can find their liberties severely curtailed. Many asylum applicants are held in detention or sent to assembly

xii Preface

camps, where conditions are austere and generally humiliating. Those who are allowed to live independently are spread throughout the country, often leading to the separation of friends and families. After being allocated to a district, they must receive special permission to leave it. Social and economic rights are also being curtailed. Few asylum- seekers in Europe have the right to work although applications often take two years to process. Some countries provide social security in kind rather than cash, and withhold it from anyone who refuses to do unpaid menial work (ICIHI 1986, 39–40).

The same report notes that decisions on refugee claims are sometimes made by untrained and inexperienced civil servants under pressure to limit the number of successful applicants. Right to counsel, right to appeal or review, and the right to a translator are routinely violated in most Western countries. Decisions have political and racial biases. In Germany, it is next to impossible for Turks and Pakistanis to get refugee status. In 1982, only twenty-six out of 12,000 Salvadorean asylum applicants were admitted in the United States. In 1985 the United States deported up to 400 Salvadoreans per month (ICIHI 1986, 40). According to an estimate by the Inter-Religious Task Force on Central America and Central American Concern, between 1980 and 1986 over 35,000 Central Americans were sent home. Groups of Tamils in Holland, Zairians in Switzerland, and Turks in Germany have also been sent home against their will (ICIHI 1986, 40).

In November 1986 an Immigration Reforms and Control Act, known as the Simpson-Radino Bill, was approved in the United States. It enabled the authorities to prosecute employers who hired illegal aliens (Alfred 1987). As the life of illegal refugees in the United States became more precarious, their flow to Canada, which until then had been famous for its relatively open refugee policy, considerably increased. Between 1 January and 15 February 1987, a total of 2294 Salvadoreans and 600 Guatemalans crossed the U.S.–Canadian border seeking political asylum. Along with some other refugees from Chile, Sri Lanka, Iran, and other countries, they made up a total of 6120 refugee claimants who came to Canada in this six-week period (*Globe and Mail*, 20 February 1987). By then, Canada had a backlog of 20,000 refugee claimants still waiting for decisions by the immigration authorities. To reduce the backlog, Canadian nongovernment organizations (NGOs) suggested a number of reforms in the status determination procedure that would make it more efficient. The government's response surprised everyone concerned with refugees. On February 1987 the Canadian government announced new measures, including transit visa requirements, for all the countries for which a visa was required. Additionally, the government proposed two new bills, c-84 and c-55, aimed at controlling swelling numbers of refugee claimants and separating bogus from genuine refugees. While in agreement about the need to prevent possible abuse of the system, refugee advocates attacked the proposed bills for their failure to provide adequate hearing to refugee claimants. While confrontations between the government and refugee advocates took place, the backlog of refugee claimants grew to 115,000 cases and was in need of urgent solution. In spite of the expressed criticisms, the proposed bills were passed and became effective in January 1989. However, the new procedures for refugee status determination proved to be costly, inefficient, and incapable of detecting "bogus" refugees. Therefore, a new bill was introduced to the Parliament on 16 June 1992. The proposed changes include elimination of one of the two existing status determination hearings, fingerprinting of all refugee claimants in order to detect and deport criminals, and granting more power to immigration officers at the border, enabling them to reject refugee claims.

Even if developed countries were more open to admitting higher numbers of refugees, resettlement to a country with a different language, culture, economic structure, and climate would, for most world refugees, not be a viable solution. Consequently, some 90 per cent of world refugees remain in countries of asylum (Cuenod 1989, 245) that are already hard hit by the economic crisis. Do refugees have any hope of becoming self-sufficient there?

REFUGEES VERSUS ECONOMIC MIGRANTS

Much debate exists around the difference between refugees and economic immigrants. A refugee is defined by the United Nations High Commission for Refugees as an individual who has left the country of origin because of a "well-founded fear of persecution" by governmental or nongovernmental forces related to race, religion, or participation in political parties/movements. The Organization of African States (OAS) found this definition too narrow and expanded it to include indirect victims of civil war and foreign intervention. The OAS definition was also adopted at the 1984 Cartagena meeting for Latin American refugees. Regardless of whether a refugee is defined in narrow or in broader terms, a refugee is believed to differ from an immigrant in two respects. First, a refugee leaves for political reasons, while an immigrant migrates for reasons related to employment. Second, a refugee is forced to abandon her or his homeland, but an immigrant makes a decision to leave based on an analysis of the costs and benefits of the move. Yet both of these distinctions have been questioned. With respect to the first, Dowty (1987, 183) observed that "so-called economic migrants are often responding as much to political repression as to material deprivation." The same is true of refugees. With respect to the second distinction, Richmond (1988) argues that most migrants would fall between two extremes: at one extreme there are those whose flight is reactive (they are forced to migrate); at the other extreme there are those whose migration is proactive (they migrate by choice).

While in reality it is difficult to draw a clearcut distinction between refugees and economic migrants, most asylum countries try to adopt a legal definition that distinguishes between the two groups. The need to separate the groups is tied to humanitarian protection and assistance. It is only to refugees that the host governments, as well as the international community, extend assistance.

UNHCR AND INTERNATIONAL NGOS

The international system of protection of and assistance to refugees was first established under the League of Nations and was reaffirmed by the United Nations Organization. In 1950 the General Assembly of the United Nations created the office of the United Nations High Commissioner for Refugees (UNHCR). Although originally created to deal with people displaced by the Second World War, UNHCR has progressively become an instrument of assistance to refugees generated by conflicts in Third World countries (Zarjevski 1988). While no country is obliged to respect principles set by UNHCR, many countries prefer to sign the 1951 UNHCR Convention and the 1967 Protocol on Refugees in order to share the burden that refugees impose on host countries. Once they become signatories to these documents, host counties may be held responsible for not respecting principles set out in these conventions, including a right to economic survival.

Until the early 1980s, UNHCR and other institutions concerned with refugees had promoted predominantly three strategies: emergency aid in camps, assistance with voluntary repatriation, and third-country resettlement. Settlement in camps was often understood as a temporary measure, to be followed by either repatriation or resettlement (Keely 1981).

By 1981 the total refugee population of the world had risen to 12.6 million. The majority of these people (8.1 million) were outside their country of origin, while the remaining 4.5 million were displaced internally (Keely 1981). Most of these people were in camps characterized by unhealthy living conditions and by inadequate security conditions. Although voluntary repatriation was regarded as the best solution, it did not seem viable because of the persistence of violence in most countries where refugees originated. At the same time, developed countries accepted only a small percentage of refugees for resettlement. Problems associated with traditional approaches to handling refugees began to emerge in the 1980s. As a result, some African governments and UNHCR devised a new strategy involving a shift of some resettlement resources from expensive third-country resettlement to local settlement in countries of first asylum. These rechannelled resources were to be directed into development projects that would make refugees economically self-sufficient in the country where they initially sought asylum (Keely 1981).

The new approach promoting local settlement was referred to as the "durable solution" model in Central America.[1] It involved the systematic and organized creation of productive activities (such as artisanal or industrial shops and medium-size farming projects) that would ensure that the refugees became economically self-sufficient, whether individually or collectively. An unpublished UNHCR memorandum outlined the advantages of the durable solution approach:

Self sufficiency projects are the ultimate aim of UNHCR as they allow the refugees to become independent of emergency assistance and be productively integrated in the receiving community. In the under-developed countries with serious unemployment problems, self-sufficiency projects offer the best alternative for the refugee's work problem. For the receiving country, these durable solutions are a contribution to the national economy, particularly the projects which include both nationals and refugees. Every durable solution is at the same time a very fruitful experience for the refugee which will become an asset when the conditions in his country of origin permit his return.

UNHCR, whose budget had swelled to $500 million in 1980, was to be essentially a catalyst and coordinator of local settlement projects carried out by governmental and nongovernmental development organizations (Cuenod 1989, 232–5).

Yet many host countries are resistant to projects involving the economic integration of refugees. Stein (1987, 56) explains this hesitancy as follows: first, local integration weakens support for struggles such as separatist movements that produce refugee flows; second, refugee groups may be too large for the host country to absorb; third, economic integration could encourage other refugees to flee to the country of asylum; fourth, host governments fear they will be accused of favouring refugees over needy nationals or of creating competition between refugees and local labour; and, fifth, governments are concerned with both the short-term and the long-term costs of offering and maintaining development assistance to refugees.

In addition, the governments of some host countries have argued that if refugees become self-sufficient while they are in exile, they will have no incentive to go back to their homeland (ICIHI 1986, 58). For these reasons, many first-asylum governments prefer to keep refugees in camps and, when they do promote local settlement, they do not permit these enterprises to become successful. As a result, assistance distributed to refugees is never generous enough to make them seem better off than the poorest members of the host society. However, when host governments give too little assistance to refugees they are criticized. As a result, receiving governments often delegate the control of assistance to humanitarian agencies whose task it becomes to keep a balance (Harrell-Bond 1986, 18–19).

When development projects fail to make refugees self-sufficient, the blame cannot be placed entirely on deliberate attempts by the host government and nongovernmental organizations (NGOs) to block their economic integration. Even when the UNHCR, NGOs, and the government try to make refugees self-sufficient, often they do not succeed. Factors that cause these assistance programs to fail need to be carefully examined.

A NEED FOR A THEORETICAL ANALYSIS
OF REFUGEE ASSISTANCE

Evaluation of refugee assistance programs is usually carried out by those who are directly involved in the delivery of assistance. As Harrell-Bond (1986, xi–xii) observes, independent critical research in the field of refugee assistance is scarce because of the commonly held assumption that humanitarian work is above question and does not need to be examined. Her own book is an important contribution to an evaluation of relief aid to Ugandan refugees in Sudan. Studies carried out by Harrell-Bond (1986), Rogge (1987), and others (Shawcross 1984; Betts 1984; Chambers 1979; Clay and Holcombe 1985; Mason and Brown 1983; Kent 1987) have certainly contributed to our understanding of refugee assistance and why it does not succeed. What is lacking in their analyses is a link to theories of development.

Refugee settlement is a development issue. Analysis of programs for refugee assistance can improve significantly when their evaluation is related to theoretical perspectives of Third World development. Most evaluations of assistance programs concentrate on specific errors and largely ignore the global economic context in which these projects are placed. Yet broader economic processes influence the viability of specific assistance programs. It is important, therefore, to analyse these broad economic tendencies, relating them to theoretical approaches that have been elaborated by students of development. This book aims to place the analysis of urban employment programs for Salvadorean refugees in Costa Rica in the framework of theories of development, especially urban development.

ASSISTANCE TO SALVADOREAN
REFUGEES IN COSTA RICA

Salvadorean refugees started arriving in Costa Rica in 1980 in response to escalating violence in their country (see chapter 1). Unlike their compatriots in Honduras, they were not placed in refugee camps. Instead, many of them received assistance, with the goal of making them self-sufficient (see chapter 2). It is for this reason that Costa Rica is often cited as a model for refugee settlement, in spite of the fact that the durable solution program has had numerous problems.

The durable solution model of refugee settlement has been practised in Costa Rica since 1981. A number of government and voluntary agencies have participated in refugee settlement. They include local branches of such international organizations as Caritas, the Episcopalian church, and the YMCA. In addition, refugees themselves formed a number of voluntary organizations in the hope of assisting their compatriots. Apart from providing emergency aid to refugees, the UNHCR has also financed most of the refugee urban projects. Financial assistance has been provided by other international NGOs as well. They include Project Counselling for Latin American Refugees, Catholic Relief Services, the Swedish Ecumenical Action, and others. To complement international organizations and national voluntary agencies, the Costa Rican government set up CONAPARE (the National Committee for Refugees) to coordinate refugee resettlement, as well as PRIMAS (Refugee Program of the Mixed Institute for Social Assistance) to distribute UNHCR emergency aid and provide other services to refugees.

A significant effort has been made to settle Salvadorean refugees in Costa Rica (see chapters 4 and 5), and considerable energy and funds were invested in this venture. The results, however, were less than satisfactory. In 1985 it became evident to the UNHCR that less than half of the 152 projects registered with government agencies were still active. Most of the others had failed.[2] Consequently, a new formula for urban projects was introduced by an International Labour Office (ILO) worker in 1985 and was accepted by the UNHCR. Prior to 1985, most urban projects were of a collective nature with an average investment of US$1700 per project member. The new program offered small donations of about US$250 to individuals to establish small businesses at home.

The new program could hardly be called a success story. Out of the forty-nine individual Salvadorean recipients interviewed as part of the present research, only eleven (22 per cent) were working full time in the occupation for which they had received the donation. Seventeen of these refugees (35 per cent) dedicated part of their time to working in this occupation, and twenty-one people (43 per cent) were not using machinery or tools they had received through the program at all.

Not all refugee projects that were still active in 1986 performed equally well. In fact, incomes earned by the beneficiaries ranged widely. Members of some projects earned more than 12,000 colones ($214) per month; others earned less than 3000 colones ($54) per month.

My objective is to understand not only why so many projects failed
but also to identify factors that made some small projects more
successful than others. The book focuses specifically on urban self-
sufficiency projects for Salvadorean refugees. The survival and success of small urban enterprises for Salvadorean refugees in Costa
Rica can be placed in the context of a broader theoretical concern in
development studies – the survival of noncapitalist forms of production in the capitalist economy.

DEBATES ON THE SURVIVAL AND SUCCESS OF PETTY COMMODITY PRODUCERS

Urban refugee enterprises can be viewed and analysed as "informal"
or as "petty commodity production." They are relatively small, not
subject to legal regulations, and they use simple technology, with
owners participating in production alongside family members,
apprentices, and a few wage-labourers. To understand how they function, it is useful to examine theoretical debates on informality and
petty commodity production.

Contrary to the expectations of orthodox liberals, modernization
theorists (Nash, Hoselitz, Levy, Hagen, and others),[3] and Marxists,
the so-called traditional or the pre-capitalist forms of production have
not been replaced by a wage economy. Instead, they have survived,
and have re-emerged with more vigour in the present developed and
developing economies (Portes, Castells, and Benton 1989). Some
researchers believe that the persistence of small urban enterprises is
temporary and that eventually they are going to be squeezed out by
the capitalist sector. According to this line of reasoning, the only
way small-scale producers can survive is by avoiding competition
wih capitalist enterprises for as long as they can. "Articulation"
theorists, in contrast, see the capitalist system itself is responsible
for their re-emergence. Those who hold the articulation perspective
attribute the survival of petty commodity producers to the functional
role they play in capital accumulation within the capitalist sector.

One shortcoming of both these approaches is that the emphasis
they place on relations between petty commodity producers and
capitalist enterprises largely ignores relations and the organization
of production *within* small urban enterprises. Yet it is these small

enterprises that play a crucial role in the adaptability of small producers to adverse conditions created by the capitalist market.

In this book I will evaluate the usefulness of the petty commodity and articulation approaches in explaining the survival and success of Salvadorean small urban enterprises in Costa Rica. Chapter 7 examines the various relations that Salvadorean petty commodity producers have with the capitalist sector and relates them to relative success among the producers. Chapter 8 turns the focus away from relations that are external to the productive unit and, instead, concentrates on the organization and relations of production with small Salvadorean businesses, viewed as "strategies of survival."

POLICY IMPLICATIONS

These theoretical questions have policy implications not only for refugee assistance programs but for those promoting the informal sector as well. If petty commodity producers are not viable in the capitalist economy, then projects that provide assistance to urban refugees to set up small businesses are merely band-aids offering no more than temporary relief. If these enterprises are viable, more assistance should be provided to them. Understanding factors that allow them to survive is important for planning assistance programs for petty commodity producers.

Acknowledgments

Many people have collaborated to help produce this book. I wish to express my gratitude to all Salvadoreans, Costa Ricans, and others who provided me with information on the settlement of Salvadorean refugees in Costa Rica. I would like to acknowledge the valuable assistance of Alfonso Valles, Julio Torres, and Gina Mora in collecting and coding these data. Tender care given to me by my Costa Rican "mother," Denny Rojas, and my Costa Rican "sister," Gina Mora, as well as the warm friendship of many Salvadoreans, and especially of Alfonso Valles, Julio Torres, Ricardo Aguilar, Edgardo Arévalo, and Edgardo Guzman, made my stay in Costa Rica most enjoyable, and indirectly affected the quality of data I collected.

I am grateful for the comments made by Alan Simmons, Malcolm Blincow, Nudith Nagata, Sergio Aguayo, and Howard Adelman. Alan Simmons's visits to Costa Rica while I was doing research were especially useful. Our conversations in Costa Rica, as well as our correspondence, helped in clarifying my research goals and strategies and gave me the needed encouragement.

I would also like to express gratitude to my two friends from Ecuador, Gilda Farrell and Carlos Larrea. Gilda's help with designing the methodology of research and Carlos's assistance with data analysis were irreplaceable.

This research would not have been carried out without the financial assistance from the Social Sciences and Humanities Research

Council of Canada and the International Development Research Centre.

Finally, financial contribution by the University of Windsor and the Social Science Federation of Canada made the publication of this book possible.

Glossary

APTARS   Association of Salvadorean Refugee Professionals and Technicians

Caja Costarricense de Seguro Social   Health Insurance Plan

CASP/Re   Centre of Social and Political Analysis for Refugees

CECAMURESA   Training Centre for Salvadorean Refugee Women

CONAPARE   National Commission for Refugees

Coordinadora   The Coordinating Agency for Salvadorean Refugees

DIGEPARE   General Directorate for Refugees

a domicilio   home delivered services

DS   durable solution employment program

EEC   European Economic Community

ICCS   Costa Rican – Salvadorean Cultural Institute

ILO   International Labour Office

IDA   Institute of Agricultural Development

IMAS   Mixed Institute of Social Assistance

INA   National Institute for Training

INHUDES   Institute of Humanism and Development of El Salvador

LS   local sesttlement employment program

maquila   subcontracting

matanza   massacre

microempresa   small business

NGO   nongovernmental organization

OARS   Office of Orientation and Assistance to Salvadorean Refugees

operario   wage-labourer

por cuenta propia   business started without financial assistance

PRIMAS   Refugee Program of the Mixed Institute for Social Assistance

PRODES   Popular Projects for Economic and Social Development

Productor   Technical and Professional Services for Salvadorean Refugees

pupusas   traditional Salvadorean stuffed tortillas

pupusería   a small restaurant specializing in pupusas

soda   a small restaurant

UNHCR   United Nations High Commission for Refugees

YMCA   Young Men's Christian Association

Keeping Heads Above Water

Introduction

In the early 1980s UNHCR and international voluntary agencies began
to settle refugees in the country of asylum. Since the majority of
refugees are found in Africa, the issue of local settlement on this
continent has received the most attention.

In 1981 the first International Conference on Assistance to Refugees in Africa (ICARA I) was held in Geneva. Many African governments were disappointed with the results: their need for additional
resources to develop their infrastructure had not been adequately
heard. At the second conference, ICARA II, in July 1984, African
governments presented two concrete projects: direct assistance to
refugees, and infrastructure projects related to the presence of refugees in the country of asylum (Cuenod 1989; Stein 1987). In 1985,
when I started preparing for a field trip to Costa Rica, the issue of
durable solutions to refugees was widely discussed among those
concerned with refugees. While much attention was given to African
countries, not much was known about how the durable solution
program ran in Central America and Mexico. I decided to fill the
gap.

HOGAR-ESCUELA

While still in Canada I read an article on Hogar-Escuela, a project
run by the YMCA where Salvadorean young men were placed in a

residence and received technical training (*Refugiados Centroamericanos*, no. 9, 1983). The report mentioned that most of the participants in the project had withdrawn from the training classes. I wanted to find out why.

A few weeks after I arrived in Costa Rica in June 1985, I located the YMCA-run residence. There were thirty young men at Hogar-Escuela, ranging in age between sixteen and thirty-two. Most of them were finishing high school. I offered to give them English classes, an offer gladly accepted by the residents and by some YMCA administrators. These classes, given three times a week, provided a perfect setting in which the young men and I could become acquainted. After class I would stay to chat with them, play guitar, and sing. It soon turned out that chatting and singing were more enjoyable for all of us than formal instruction, so the classes stopped. From that time on, I came to the residence to socialize. I shared their meals, they taught me some songs, and I taught them a few. Then we went out to concerts and plays, dancing and drinking. In Hogar-Escuela I met some of their friends who came to visit. Gradually I started interviewing them about their participation in the project and their sociocultural integration into Costa Rican life.

FIRST ENCOUNTER WITH PATERNALISM

An informal UNHCR report entitled 'Development Approaches to Refugee Situation' specified that 'in all phases of a refugee problem it is important that the beneficiaries of projects be involved in their planning, management, and implementation as much and as soon as possible' (quoted by Cuenod 1989, 235). While most refugee-assisting agencies would agree with this statement in theory, their treatment of refugees is often paternalistic.

During my interview with the YMCA project director in San José, I told him that some young men in Hogar-Escuela had wanted me to give them classes of English. His response surprised me. "We don't want them to study English," he said, "because we invest so much into their training here and then they learn English and leave for Canada; we want them to stay here." This statement was contradictory in two ways: first, the Costa Rican government would have preferred that all or most Salvadoreans left for Canada; and, second, the resources spent on refugee training were not provided by the local YMCA but were received from international sources. I was most surprised, however, not by the director's ignorance but by his paternalism: what mattered to him was not what the young men had wanted me to do but what he felt about it. His response did not prevent me from giving classes, but it gave me the first taste of paternalistic treatment by workers in refugee assistance agencies.

This first impression was reinforced in my interviews with participants in the Hogar-Escuela project. They told me that initially young Salvadorean refugees were encouraged to form various committees, but that almost all the decisions taken by these committees were overturned by the YMCA representatives. Eventually, the members felt it was useless to maintain the committees and, consequently, they disbanded.

The Salvadoreans also told me how they were prevented from taking arts, crafts, and theatre courses from Salvadorean teachers. Education in Hogar-Escuela had been provided by Salvadorean teachers until a decree was proclaimed prohibiting foreign teachers from working. Salvadorean teachers had to leave their jobs and their students were sent to INA (National Training Institute) and placed in one of three courses – carpentry, tailoring, and electrical training – often against their will. This coersion explained the high drop-out rate.

A psychologist used to come to the residence every day, yet most of the time he sat in a room by himself. Despite the fact that many young men living in the residence needed some psychological counselling or at least someone to talk to, they did not go to see him. The psychologist used to tell the boys they were "subversives." He scolded them for not going to church and, when his advice was solicited, he provided ridiculous explanations for their "unusual" behaviour. When he was asked by one of the boys to explain his supposed premonitions, the psychologist asked him if he had witches in his family. He suggested to another boy, who used to draw sad female faces, that he had homosexual tendencies.

Most of the boys who lived in this residence acquired a feeling of mistrust towards the Costa Rican agencies that implemented the projects. After the residence was closed in December 1985, they preferred to work illegally than to apply to agencies for assistance.

BARRIO JESUS

In the summer of 1985 I also began conducting interviews with representatives of agencies assisting refugees. At the Episcopalian church office I met Salvadoreans who had received aid from this agency. They resided in Barrio Jesus, a semi-urban settlement where a number of Salvadorean families rented houses. One of the men I met at the office introduced me to other Salvadorean residents of Barrio Jesus. I started interviewing them about their relations with Costa Ricans as well as about their participation in durable solution projects. I found out that administering a refugee assistance project is a complex affair that requires expertise in business administration, agronomy, economics, psychology, and sociology. Without this expertise, agencies in charge of refugee assistance committed many mistakes. Projects could not reach self-sufficiency and, consequently, many refugees had to abandon them.

THE LOS ANGELES PROJECT

At the end of the summer my thesis adviser, Alan Simmons, came to Costa Rica with his wife Jean Turner. We decided to visit Nicaraguan refugee camps and some Salvadorean rural projects. We arranged to visit two Savadorean projects. The first was the Los Angeles farm, administered by the Refugee Program of the Mixed Institute for Social Assistance (PRIMAS). The second was another farm that had just been leased by Econo-Agro, to which twelve families from the Los Angeles farm had been relocated. I had read a great deal about the Los Angeles farm, the biggest Costa Rican rural project for refugees (see chapter 3).

We found that the same kind of paternalism I had encountered in Hogar-Escuela characterized agencies in charge of Los Angeles. At first the project was administered by the Red Cross, and then it passed to PRIMAS. Salvadoreans formed various committees in the Los Angeles project. Similar to their young compatriots, they soon realized that they had no decision-making power. Everything was controlled by Costa Rican administrators. In 1981 a UNHCR representative was quoted in a newspaper article as saying: "We want to give the refugees participation little by little. But the refugees feel that those who make the decisions, administer funds, and supervise the camp either live in the capital or, like the Red Cross workers, have isolated themselves within the camp" (*Tico Times*, 14 August 1981). The same article made reference to the misuse of funds and the inequitable distribution of goods by the Red Cross. The following incident was reported:

In December [1980], when the camp was moved from Murcielago to Los Angeles, one of the large gas stoves the refugees had been using was appropriated "temporarily" by the 18 Red Cross workers for their head-quarters, even though the post was already equipped with a small stove … [On 18 July] five women … went up to the Red Cross post to ask for it. Failing to get a positive response, they called their husbands. A bitter exchange followed, and one of the refugees tried to take the stove. The Red Cross called in the Rural Guard, later charging that there had been a "mutiny" in the camp. The arrival of 13 armed Guardsmen, who stayed overnight and half the next day, terrified the refugees, many of whom had witnessed massacres of family or village members by uniformed men in their own country.

When I visited in 1985, the farm was run by a Costa Rican agronomist who assigned tasks to be performed in the field to project members. If the agronomist was not in the field, refugees did not know what to do and, at times, returned to their barracks. There were no more refugee committees. Most of the project members did not care whether the farm prospered or failed. Refugees who had been relocated from Los Angeles to the other farm we visited confirmed the impression we had formed about Los Angeles.

FINDING SMALL URBAN ENTERPRISES

In May 1986 I returned to Costa Rica to continue research on durable solution programs for Salvadorean refugees. I decided to focus on urban projects. I obtained lists of all urban projects implemented by agencies assisting Salvadorean refugees. Instead of selecting a sample, I tried to locate all of them with the help of my assistant Alfonso. Lists of projects I received from the agency had addresses. In some cases, these addresses were not exact (instead of walking 200 meters to the west we might have to walk 300 meters to the east from a particular food store), but by asking people in the vicinity we could easily find the projects in question. However, some workshops had changed their location without informing the agency administering them. The only way to find these projects was through social networks, particularly my Salvadorean friends. Their assistance was especially valuable in the search for projects that had failed (since no one from the agencies in charge knew where their former members resided) and for small urban enterprises that received no institutional assistance. All together, we found sixty-seven active projects (out of the 119 implemented), thirty-five projects that had failed, and eight small enterprises that received no institutional assistance.

EARNING THE TRUST OF INFORMANTS

To most informants I was a stranger. How could I convince them to allow me to interview them? How could I make them trust me and give me honest answers? These problems are often faced in any research involving human beings, and particularly in urban research because of the anonymity of its environment. To complicate my situation, refugees in general, because of their past experience of persecution, are suspicious of people who ask many questions. Besides, Salvadorean refugees working in projects view researchers with mistrust because they have been "over-interviewed" by Costa Rican undergraduate student researchers and agency representatives. They feel that student researchers only waste their time and that nothing good ever comes out of it. When agency representatives come to interview them, project members feel they may decide to take away their machinery. I tried solving this problem by having a Salvadorean assistant conduct all interviews together with me. On occasion I asked some of my Salvadorean friends to come along with me if project members happened to be their friends or kin. This made a great difference in response. Coming with a Salvadorean friend or assistant was the same as saying, "I am on your side. I would like to do something that would help refugees in the future." It was also much easier to "break the ice" and allow our conversation to flow beyond the questions included in the interview schedule.

There was another way I tried to earn the trust of my informants. There are some differences in vocabulary between Salvadoreans and Costa Ricans (see chapter 3). Usually, Salvadoreans use the Costa

Rican vocabulary with Costa Ricans and with others who are not part of their community. As you become their friend, you are introduced to the Salvadorean way of speaking. When a researcher uses this vocabulary with a respondent, a symbolic link between the two is established. This indicates that the researcher is genuinely interested in learning about the community under study and identifies with the problems faced by its members. My use of Salvadorean expressions did not have any practical significance, for we could have understood each other speaking *tico* (the Costa Rican dialect). It did, however, help in establishing an atmosphere of trust with my informants.

INCONSISTENT AND INCOMPLETE DATA

While these techniques help make collected data more reliable, they nevertheless fail to solve one problem: people do not always remember all the required information and, even when they have no intention of misrepresenting facts, they nonetheless do so. This problem is especially acute in studies trying to measure economic variables, such as income, sales, and investments. It was certainly the case in my research, since I found considerable discrepancies in the reported data.

For instance, often respondents could not estimate their monthly sales or investment in raw materials. In these cases, we asked them to give an approximate number of units sold per week, the price of each unit, and the cost of raw materials used to produce a unit. As an example, a tailor was asked how many pants and how many shirts he made per week, how much he sold each unit for, and how much he had to invest in raw materials (fabrics, buttons, zippers) to produce a pair of pants and a shirt.

When I reviewed questionnaires after having done interviews, I found some inconsistencies. Sometimes, reported sales were too low to cover even salaries paid to wage-labourers or to correspond (after the deduction of business expenses) to the reported salaries of enterprise owners. Sometimes, reported sales seemed exaggerated. In most cases I relied on the information on sales and business expenses to do the necessary calculations of monthly incomes, but in some cases I had to ignore them and trust the information on salaries. Every detail relating to the qualitative information on the business (such as the type of accommodation lived in, occupation of other family members, assistance received from relatives or from other agencies) added to the project in question and allowed me to estimate income derived from it quantitatively.

Project participants did not always remember the price of the machinery donated to them by the agency administering the project. In some cases, members in charge of business administration had left the project, and those remaining did not know the details of the financing, although they did usually remember the total amount. In this case, I had to estimate the value of their machinery on the basis of my knowledge of prices reported by informants in other projects.

To deal with the problem of incomplete or incorrect information, the interviewer must complement this method of data collection by informal conversation (in a situation where informants are more likely to accept the researcher), participant observation, and collection of gossip (a favourite anthropological technique of data gathering). However, in an urban environment, unless the interviewer is involved in the study of a relatively segregated community such as a slum, it is difficult to get access to networks of people controlling such information. This access can be gained through friends from the community under study. Making friends, however, is not an easy task. It requires the "right" circumstances and considerable investment in time and favours. One interview with an informant about his or her business does not allow for friendship to develop. I did have certain advantages in this area, however, because of my experience in the YMCA residence in the summer of 1985.

San José and Heredia (where most of my research took place) are small cities. Friends and acquaintances constantly run into one another in the street, as happened to my assistants and friends when we were together. Through these accidental encounters I gained access to additional information on projects, on the employment situation of persons with whom we were conversing, and on other issues related to the life of Salvadoreans in Costa Rica.

I was often invited to dinners and parties, for drinks, or to other social gatherings by and through my friends. These occasions provided opportunities to expand my understanding of Costa Rican refugee employment programs and their implementation, as well as the Salvadorean community in Costa Rica as a whole.

CONCEPTUALISING AND MEASURING SUCCESS

The major objective of my research was to measure the relative success of Salvadorean small urban enterprises. How was I to measure it? A review of the literature of small urban enterprises suggested that three variables could be used: monthly income, capital accumulation, and increases in sales. While the first reflects the state of the enterprise at the time of the interview, the other two demonstrate the progressive improvement or deterioration of the project.

Monthly income could be calculated by subtracting the costs of raw materials, rent, utilities, debts, salaries, and amortisation of capital per month from the monthly volume of sales. However, thus measured, monthly income would not reflect any variability in time devoted to business. After I conducted several interviews, it became clear that while some refugees worked full time, others worked only part time in their own business and part or full time elsewhere, and yet others worked part time in their businesses only. It is obviously erroneous to compare the income of someone who works full time with that of a part-time worker. However, converting total incomes into hourly incomes is not a good solution either. Let us examine four hypothetical cases.

A is a shoemaker. He sells his product to several small storekeepers who like his shoes and, if he could produce more, would be glad to buy more from him. He works fifty hours a week, making 2500 colones weekly or 50 colones per hour.

B is a baker. She and her daughter live in a poor neighbourhood. Her neighbours buy her pastries, but the demand is low. She works twenty hours per week, earning 1000 colones weekly or 50 colones per hour. She would like to work more, but she knows she would not be able to sell more.

C is a seamstress. She works thirty hours per week because she also has to take care of the house and children. She earns 1500 colones per week or 50 colones per hour. It is not much in total, but she does not worry because her husband earns 2000 colones weekly as a wage-labourer.

D is a painter. He had just started his business and he does not have many customers yet. Last week he worked only 10 hours in his business and earned 500 colones. He cannot live on this money, so he continues working as a wage-labourer in construction, just as he did before he received assistance from an agency. He hopes that his business will pick up soon and he will be able to work full time.

All four business owners earn 50 colones per hour. However, only A and C are working as much as they can. B and D suffer from lack of demand and, therefore, their businesses cannot be considered as successful as those of A and C. The case of A differs from the case of C. Whereas A does enjoy good demand for his product, C does not know whether she would be able to sell more if she produced more. Cases B and D are not similar either. B earns very little and cannot support herself and her daughter on this income. She may decide to leave her business and work as a domestic helper instead. D, in contrast, already has a job that does not interfere with his own business. As the clientele expands, he will leave his salaried job.

To deal with this problem, I decided to adjust monthly income for those producers or business owners who chose to work fewer hours or whose business, I felt, could easily increase in a few months. As I believed it was normal for small business owners in Costa Rica to work forty-five hours per week (eight hours Monday through Friday, and five hours on Saturday), the adjusted monthly income could be calculated in the following way:

$$\text{Adjusted monthly income} = \frac{45 \times \text{monthly income}}{\text{Amount of hours worked per week}}$$

Income of those small enterprise owners who suffered from insufficient demand was left as reported. For small producers who worked fewer than forty-five hours (because they needed to take care of children, for instance) but who would also possibly face a problem of insufficient demand even if they produced more, income was calculated as an average between the real and the adjusted income. Monthly income, thus adjusted, became a better indicator of how well the business was doing.

What about the other two indicators of relative success: capital accumulation and increase in sales? How well do they reflect the status of a business? At times, small producers miscalculate their potential and a purchase of expensive equipment may translate into their assuming a high debt that is difficult for them to repay. This

debt may be ruinous for the business. Furthermore, although productivity may increase with the purchase of more or improved
machinery, there may be no rise in demand and, consequently, most
of the sales are channelled into paying off the debt. Such investment
does not make the business more successful.

Measuring the relative success of businesses by increases in sales
can also be problematic. Can we say that a project that started with
a volume of monthly sales of 80,000 colones and that by 1986 had
increased it to 120,000 colones (that is, by 50 per cent) is less
successful than one, with the same number of members, that at the
beginning generated 40,000 colones in sales but in 1986 was selling
as much as the first project (thus increasing its sales by 200 per
cent)? The obvious answer is no.

At a more general level, lack of improvement does not necessarily
mean that the project is not doing well. As Peattie (1982, 215)
contends:

The fact that some firms may operate comfortably at a stable level, without
growing, is fairly self-evident. However, it seems worth making the point,
in view of the tendency of some writers to adopt a tone in which it would
appear that only those enterprises with "growth potential" are worth
thinking about. Perhaps we should not sneer too much even at the one-man
shoe-making shop whose proprietor told me he had been seventeen years at
the task and that it was a "good occupation."

Since neither capital accumulation nor increase in sales reflects
relative success in small business, I decided to measure it by only
one variable – adjusted monthly income. My aim was to identify
factors that explained why some Salvadorean enterprises had gone
out of business and why incomes in the still existing projects ranged
widely. I was especially interested in finding out whether the variability in income was related to the type of relations small urban
producers had with the capitalist sector, as the "petty commodity
production" approach would lead us to believe.

PART ONE

Departure and Arrival

1 El Salvador:
Why a Refugee Movement?

More than one in four Salvadoreans were displaced as a result of the 1980–92 civil war. Almost half a million fled to internal refugee camps in San Salvador, and more than one million abandoned the country in search of safe haven elsewhere.

This situation is not unique to El Salvador. In the last decade Central America has gone through political turmoil that displaced between two and three million people. In 1981 the exodus of Guatemalans to Honduras, Mexico, the United States, and Nicaragua began. Most were indigenous peasants who had seen their villages destroyed by the military's counterinsurgency campaign. At the same time, thousands of Nicaraguans, opposed to the Sandinista government and its policies, escaped to Costa Rica and the United States. Mexico has provided asylum for the largest numbers of Central American refugees: between 300,000 and 400,000 Guatemalans and Salvadoreans are found in this country. Additionally, hundreds of thousands of other Central Americans move through Mexico on their way to the North (Zolberg, Suhrke, and Aguayo 1989, 210–20). Salvadorean refugees constitute a significant part of the Central American exodus.

MASSIVE VIOLATIONS OF HUMAN RIGHTS

Throughout history, Salvadorean people have experienced violence, but the 1980s were especially bloody. The civil war took more than

70,000 lives. Most of those killed were unarmed civilians who fell prey to the army, security forces, or death squads. The first three years of the war were the cruelest and resulted in 42,000 deaths. Excessive brutality was reported by numerous witnesses. The *Report on Human Rights in El Salvador* (1983) states that 40 out of 406 victims of repression were beaten to death, decapitated, hung, or had their throats slit. Many *campesinos* (peasants) died as a result of genocide-like counter-insurgency campaigns consisting of heavy aerial bombing followed by on-the-ground "clean-up." The same report claims that during the August 1982 military campaign in San Vicente, between three and four hundred villagers were massacred. In addition, many were abducted and "disappeared." Between May and December 1982, 451 individuals were abducted. Eighty per cent of them (363 victims) "disappeared," forty-two were imprisoned by the Ministry of Justice, and forty-six were held by the army and security forces.

What explanations can be given for so much violence in this tiny country? Root causes of political repression lie in the extreme economic inequality. A testimony of one Salvadorean peasant in a Honduran refugee camp offers an illustration of the links between political repression and economic conditions among the Salvadorean poor:

We would go to the coffee plantations, and the wages were unfair. We would go to the cotton plantations and the situation was even worse, and it was the same in the sugar cane fields; the salary was just a token and our children were naked.

We couldn't find work because the land was in the hands of just a few who had it ... In the face of this, the people got organised and said, "Now we are going to protest, because the way things are is not just. We want bread and we want our lives to be respected." But they answered us with death, with a great repression. Instead of trying to find solutions to our problems, they acted like criminals.

So it got to the point that they would go looking for us where we stayed, in our houses, during the day and at night; the guardsmen, the soldiers and the para-military forces would come. One day, they came looking for all the men in my town; they came inside my house but they didn't find me. Then they wanted to kill my daughter and my wife ... My wife and my daughter were so horrified after this, that they never stayed at our house again. We all fled to the bushes (Camarda 1985, 8).

In the decade preceding the civil war, poverty levels became alarming in El Salvador. In 1975, 40.9 per cent of rural families had no land. Eighty per cent of the population of El Salvador earned less than enough to subsist (Burke 1976, 480–1). Land distribution became extremely skewed. Holdings of 100 hectares and more constituted only 0.7 per cent of all agricultural farms but took up 39 per cent of all the agricultural land (Colindres 1976). What led to this situation?

HISTORICAL BACKGROUND

The Spanish conquest of El Salvador introduced diseases that killed many Indian peasants. Those who survived were pushed off their lands and forced to work in the newly established estates. From this time on, the history of land holding in El Salvador was characterized by massive dispossession of the peasantry and concentration of land in the hands of large estate owners. By 1821, when El Salvador became independent, one-third of the total land area was concentrated in 400 large haciendas (Montgomery 1982, 38).

In the mid nineteenth century, El Salvador's republican government pursued a policy that encouraged commercial agriculture by increasing the range of commercial crops. Communal lands, owned by the indigenous communities (*ejidos*) and devoted to subsistence agriculture, were perceived as an obstacle to economic development. As the commercial importance of coffee became apparent, the government decided to change the existing structure of land tenure by abolishing communal lands. The first measure that led to the abolition was the decree of 1856, which stated that unless two-thirds of the communal lands were planted in coffee they would be appropriated by the state (Montgomery 1982, 40). A 1879 decree gave title to land to any cultivator on the *ejido* who planted one-quarter of his plot in coffee, cocoa, rubber, and agave plants. The decree did not specify membership in a village community as a prerequisite to obtaining the title. This made it possible for *haciendados* (hacienda owners) to encroach on communal properties. Attempts were made by villagers to comply with the new legislation by converting the *ejido* lands to the cultivation of plants producing export crops. Costs of coffee planting, however, were too great for the villagers, especially since they had no credit available to them during the five-year period needed for coffee plants to mature (Browning 1971, 181–9).

The government of Rafael Zaldivar was convinced that the *ejidos* were an obstacle to progress and that rapid development of commercial agriculture could only be achieved if communally owned land was held as private property. In February 1881, therefore, *tierras comunales* (communal lands) were abolished. They were divided among those who used it as *comuneros* (communal land holders), tenants, or under any other agreement.

The implementation of the law was accompanied by confusion and corruption. Many landowners claimed parts of the communal land they had occupied before 1881. There were ample opportunities for arbitrary and illegal usurpation of property. The law stated that titles to land had to be registered within six months of the abolition of communal lands. Since illiterate villagers could not always understand the stipulations of the new law and sometimes lost their legitimate possessions, many rich landowners benefited from the new law, often through bribery of appointed officials (Browning 1971, 204–12).

Abolition of *tierras comunales* marked the first stage in the massive dispossession of small producers. Once that step was undertaken, others followed. The world financial crisis of 1914–22 and the postwar depression brought about the decline of coffee prices, difficulties in shipping, and a reduction in the value of land. Small farmers lost their business to large hacienda owners whose wealth was secure. Lending policies established by the major banks favoured large farmers. It was virtually impossible for small cultivators to obtain credit (Montgomery 1982, 45).

Because of the decline in coffee prices during the Great Depression, Salvadorean agriculturalists began to cultivate cotton. Large areas of the Pacific lowlands were converted to this new crop. As well, many large estates started growing sugar for export. Because of these developments, the economic value of land increased and, consequently, many small tenants and sharecroppers (*colones* and *aparceros*, respectively) were pushed off the land and converted into wage-labourers (Durham 1979, 44).

POLITICAL STRUGGLE AND REPRESSION

This massive dispossession of the peasants provoked them to react. The first documented peasant uprising in El Salvador took place in

1832, led by Anastacio Aquino, an Indian *cacique* (headman). Government forces crushed the 3000-person uprising a year after it started and decapitated the leader (Montgomery 1982, 39–40).

A hundred years later, in 1932, the second peasant revolt took place in the western highlands, which were hard hit by the world economic crisis. The Communist party, led by Augustin Farabundo Marti, began to prepare for the rebellion in 1930 through the Regional Federation of Salvadorean Workers. To contain the movement, President Pio Romero Bosque banned demonstrations, rallies, and leftist propaganda. When his decree was ignored, several hundred *campesinos* were imprisoned. Between mid November 1930 and late February 1931, about twelve hundred people were thrown in jail for political activities. Demonstrations and strikes continued, however, and an uprising was scheduled for 22 January 1932. This plan became known to the government, and Marti, together with his two supporters, was arrested. Without leadership, the revolt turned out to be disorganized and uncoordinated. Peasant attacks were easily repelled by security forces. Within three days, the insurrection was suppressed, followed by a *matanza* (massacre) directed mainly at the Indians. Anyone in Indian dress was likely to be assaulted by security forces. An estimated 30,000 people were massacred after the uprising (Montgomery 1982, 50–3). This *matanza* had a tremendous political significance for the revolutionary struggle in El Salvador, and became an important symbol of martyrdom.

Following the insurrection, *campesino* unions and all other political organizations were outlawed (Montgomery 1982, 53). Any movement that challenged the existing system was labelled communist and subversive (North 1985, 40).

Accelerated urbanization in the 1960s and 1970s led to the growth of the working and middle classes, which in turn demanded political reform. They organized unions and staged strikes. Students formed associations and opposition parties. Political democratization in the cities contrasted with continuing repression of peasant unions. Until the mid 1960s any mention of peasant unions was taboo (North 1985, 43–58). In 1965, when the first peasant organization since the *matanza* was formed, the landed elite responded by establishing their own organization, called ORDEN (Democratic National Organization). Although formed in secrecy around 1961, this organization became public in 1968. One of its objectives was to recruit in every village.

The National Guard was ready to provide training to ORDEN members and to all new members ORDEN managed to recruit (North 1985, 71).

In the 1970s urban social movements continued to grow: unions organized strikes, students demonstrated, and peasants put pressure on the government to introduce agrarian reform. By 1975 three left-wing guerrilla organizations had been established to coordinate popular opposition (North 1985, 77).

The government thereupon increased its repression of all political bodies, including the church. Father Rutilio Grande was assassinated on 12 March 1977 and became the first Salvadorean religious martyr. His assassination was followed by the murder of Father Alfonso Navarro. Several other murders of priests who defended human rights and organized peasants into rural cooperatives could be cited, but the most important of all was the assassination of Monsignor Oscar Romero, the archbishop of San Salvador, on 24 March 1979 (North 1985, 74–6).

By the late 1970s the repression had reached an astounding scale. The Carter administration, fearing that the brutality would provoke a revolution, supported a coup d'état that replaced the repressive government of General Romero by a military-civilian junta on 15 October 1979. This coup, while producing the appearance of "democratization," did not put an end to violence. Civilians in the junta did not have any power. By 1981 all of them had resigned to protest the escalation of violence by security forces and paramilitary organizations (North 1985, 80–1).

AGRARIAN REFORM AND THE CIVIL WAR

The junta was faced with a need for agrarian reform. Several land reforms were introduced between 1932 and 1960s, but their objectives were moderate. They included distribution of government-owned land among small producers and limited provision of credit, fertilizers, and housing. Expropriation from large landowners for redistribution was never considered. In fact, it was ruled unconstitutional. The amount of land offered to the producers through these earlier reforms was at times so small that a family could not subsist on it. With virtually no credit, small producers often could not pay the rent and had to sell their plots. The measures therefore failed to resolve problems of land shortage among small producers (Browning

1971, 273–92). Agrarian reform became a burning issue after the 1969 expulsion of 30,000 Salvadoreans from Honduras. Immigrants returning home found that 58 per cent of agricultural workers were either unemployed or underemployed (North 1985, 65).

On 6 March 1980 the government of El Salvador announced plans for agrarian reform to be carried out in three phases. The first phase consisted of expropriation of 80 per cent of the lands in estates larger than 500 hectares which would be converted into rural cooperatives. The second phase aimed at redistributing the land of the 150–500-hectare plots owned by the coffee oligarchy. Tenants of small plots would become land owners under the third phase of the reform.

Neither the second nor the third phase were ever carried out. A stage of siege was declared on 5 March 1980, preceding the announcement of the Basic Agrarian Reform Law, thus allowing for the militarization of the country made possible by generous military aid from the United States (North 1985, 90–2). Many potential beneficiaries of the reform fled their homes for fear of violence from old landowners and military forces (Simon and Stephens 1981, 175). The Legal Aid Office of the Archdiocese of San Salvador reported that peasant settlements were invaded 380 times by the military in the first six months of 1980, resulting in the burning and destruction of peasant houses. More than 200 peasant cooperative leaders were reported killed in 1980 (North 1985, 85–6). At least ninety leaders of peasant organizations and a large number of potential beneficiaries were killed during 1981 (*Evolución Económica de las Reformas* 1982, 513). Areas of greater concentration of small renters – Chalatenango, Cuscatlan, and Morazan – were victimized by the military and security forces. The majority of the 75,000 people who were displaced from these areas would have been beneficiaries of the program (Simon and Stephens 1981, 176).

INTERNAL AND EXTERNAL MOVEMENTS OF REFUGEES

As a result of violent attacks on their lives and the destruction of their economic base, Salvadoreans began to flee from their towns and villages. The first massive internal migration of displaced people started in January 1980, when 2000 peasants sought refuge in Las Vueltas, Chalatenango, as a result of violence directed at them by

Table 1
Location and Numbers of Salvadorean Refugees and Displaced Persons, 1985

Country	Legally recognized	Illegal	Total
El Salvador (displaced persons)	269,311	195,000	464,131
Honduras	18,000	2,000	20,000
Guatemala		70,000	70,000
Nicaragua	17,500		17,500
Costa Rica	10,000		10,000
Mexico		120,000	120,000
United States		250,000	250,000
Belize	2,000	5,000	7,000
Total	316,631	642,000	958,631

Source: *Out of the Ashes* (1985), based on statistics provided by the UNHCR, the Government Commission for the Displaced People of El Salvador, estimates on illegal refugees made by agency and church workers, and the Inter-Religious Task Force on Central America.

members of ORDEN. By the end of 1980, the number of displaced people had risen to 75,000 (Montes 1986, 5–6). At the same time, a massive international refugee migration began which, by 1985, had reached half a million. According to some estimates (see table 1), most of them (some 250,000 people) settled in the United States illegally and were subject to deportation at any moment. Significant numbers of Salvadoreans (some 120,000) fled to Mexico, most of whom did not have legal status there either, although their presence in the country was tolerated. The same was true of 70,000 Salvadoreans in Guatemala. Some 20,000 refugees were interned in Honduran refugee camps, which were characterized by dismal security conditions and intimidation by the Honduran army. Other Salvadorean refugees were found in Costa Rica, Nicaragua, Belize, Panama, Canada, and Australia.

Since it is difficult to estimate a mobile refugee population, especially in the case of illegal refugees, some of these figures can be questioned. According to the *University for Peace* (1985), for instance, there were 180,000 and not 70,000 Salvadoreans in Guatemala. The same source quotes another publication (*Seeking Safe Haven: A Congressional Guide to Helping Central American Refugees in the United States*) that evaluated the Salvadorean population in the United States as being between 689,000 and 754,000 in 1984.

According to Montes (1986), approximately one million Salvadorean lived in the United States. While table 1 gives an estimate of 10,000 Salvadorean refugees in Costa Rica, according to other sources (discussed in chapter 2) there were some 6000 Salvadorean refugees there in 1985.

By talking to many Salvadoreans not only in Costa Rica but also in Canada, I formed an impression that refugees choose a country of asylum on the basis of their personal economic situation. The poorest of them fled to internal refugee camps. Those who could afford to pay a bus fare and food for a few days or even weeks moved to the neighbouring countries – Honduras, Guatemala, and Nicaragua. Those who could afford a plane ticket fled to Mexico, Costa Rica, and the United States. Some refugees went to Mexico and Costa Rica by bus, but this long journey also required considerable savings. Although most Salvadoreans identified ideologically with the Sandinistas in Nicaragua and were welcomed there, fear of conscription for their children and hardships imposed by the civil war discouraged many from staying there.

2 Costa Rica as a Country of Asylum

Costa Rica has a long-established humanitarian tradition as a country of asylum for individual refugees fleeing repressive régimes in Chile, Argentina, and other South American countries. Its first experience with the massive refugee flow began early in 1979 with the arrival of approximately 50,000 Nicaraguans fleeing persecution by the Somoza government. In July 1979, when the Somoza régime was overthrown and the Sandinista government installed, most of these people went back to their own country.

Shortly after the Nicaraguans withdrew from Costa Rica, Salvadorean refugees began to move there. In May 1980, two hundred Salvadoreans occupied the Costa Rican embassy in San Salvador, asking for political asylum. This event marked the beginning of the massive refugee flow from El Salvador to Costa Rica. By 1983 the number of Salvadoreans residing in Costa Rica had reached approximately 15,000, two-thirds of whom were receiving UNHCR assistance. In the same year, some 250 Cubans occupied the Peruvian embassy in Havana and were given asylum by Costa Rica. The flow of refugees from Guatemala to Costa Rica started in 1981 but was never numerically significant. Beginning in 1983, a new wave of Nicaraguans arrived.

Various sources differ in their estimates of the refugee population in Costa Rica. According to CONAPARE (National Commission for

Table 2
Distribution of Refugees in Costa Rica by Country of Origin, 1985

Country of Origin	Number	Percentage
Nicaragua	10,250	54.0
El Salvador	6,112	32.0
Cuba	2,385	13.0
Guatemala	172	0.9
Honduras	77	0.4
Chile	20	0.1
Total	19,008	100.0

Source: MIDEPLAN (1985)

Refugees), a government agency in charge of refugees, there were about 19,000 refugees in 1985. Their distribution by country of origin is presented in table 2.

According to UNHCR, in 1985 there were 17,000 refugees in the country, 12,153 of whom were receiving UNHCR emergency aid. In the same year, the Refugee Office of the General Immigration Department identified 14,866 refugees (*University for Peace* 1985, 145). This discrepancy possibly arises from the fact that the UNHCR does not have information on the departure of refugees to third countries of resettlement. The CONAPARE estimate seems to be inflated, either because of a deliberate strategy to exaggerate the problem or because of a mistake by the author of the report. In a different source (*University for Peace* 1985, 145), CONAPARE was quoted as giving the figure of 25,000 refugees in the country, of whom 15,000 had legal documents. The figure of 15,000 legal refugees is closer to the estimate by the Immigration Department.

An estimate for 1986 was 30,466 refugees: 21,495 Nicaraguans, 6170 Salvadoreans, 2499 Cubans, 190 Guatemalans, 27 Chileans, 19 Hondurans, and 66 refugees from other countries (*Contra Punto*, 2 November 1986). Newspapers also cited a figure of 210,000 illegal foreigners (*La Nación*, 22 September 1986).

IMMIGRATION LAWS AND STATUS DETERMINATION PROCEDURES

In August 1977, Costa Rica signed the 1951 UN Convention and the 1967 UN Protocol on Refugees. It was not until October 1980, however, that enabling legislation defining criteria for refugee status was produced and put into practice. By that date, there were already 2500 Salvadorean refugees in the country, all of whom had entered as "tourists."

As such, they had to present a return ticket and deposit US$150 per person. The tourist visa was valid for only thirty days. To have it renewed, an applicant had again to present a return ticket, an additional US$150 per person, and a doctor's certificate. This visa was given for six months, during which the applicant was not allowed to work. After the tourist visa had expired, a foreigner was allowed to apply for resident status. Applications for resident status had to be accompanied by a work permit which, in turn, depended on the applicant showing evidence of a job offer. If the work permit was denied by the Ministry of Labour, no residency was granted.

This procedure presented a serious problem for refugees, because the great majority did not have the necessary financial means. The procedure was long and required hiring a lawyer, paying for medical examinations and photographs, and other expenses. Moreover, while under review, the applicant was still not allowed to work. Often, by the time residency was granted, the original employment offer was no longer available, yet the applicant could not accept another job since residency status was based on the original offer. Consequently, when some applicants were found to be working in other jobs, they lost their residency.

Given these difficulties, it is hardly surprising that before 1980 many refugees lived in irregular migratory conditions that made them vulnerable and subject to deportation if caught by immigration officials. On 15 October 1980, for instance, while some Salvadoreans were celebrating a mass commemorating the death of their martyrs at the Cathedral of San José, immigration and National Security officers entered the cathedral and arrested twenty-six of them for lack of proper documents. Two of them were later deported (*Derechos Humanos en Centroamérica* 1981, 9).

With the passage of the refugee bill in October 1980, Salvadoreans could apply for refugee status under UNHCR criteria that demanded that an applicant show evidence of a "well-founded fear of persecution" and, because of this fear, could not enjoy the protection of her or his country (*Estudio Sobre la Situación Jurídica de Asilados, Refugiados y Personas Desplazadas* 1983, 9). Following the decree, CONAPARE (National Commission for Refugees) was created and was defined as a "permanent body responsible for creation of programmes and coordination action for refugees who have come or are arriving in the country." CONAPARE's mandate, as defined by the December 1982 decree, included the following responsibilities:

1 to develop policies for refugees dictated by the National Security Council;
2 to define policies necessary to develop programs and projects for refugees to be followed by government bodies as well as by international and national voluntary agencies working in the field;
3 to coordinate and supervise the work of all institutions participating in programmes and projects for refugees; and
4 to maintain coordination with governmental bodies in charge of defining legal aspects related to refugees.

After the refugee law was introduced, UNHCR was placed in charge of reviewing individual applications for refugee status and submitting them to the National Immigration Council. The council assumed this function in May 1981. By that time the number of Salvadoreans in Costa Rica had surpassed 6000, and it was decided to use a procedure based on a group recognition of refugees. The National Immigration Council, in coordination with CONAPARE, established a commission located at the Costa Rican Red Cross to grant refugee identification cards to all Salvadoreans who had abandoned their country after 1 May 1980. This procedure was in place until December 1981, when it was replaced by the individual refugee determination procedure. Some Salvadoreans preferred not to apply under the individual system for fear of possible persecution following their testimony.[1]

Even though the UNHCR Convention and Protocol on Refugees, signed by Costa Rica in 1977, sets up a principle of *non-refoulement* (nondeportation), harassment of Salvadorean refugees by immigration officers and subsequent deportations were frequent, especially in the first few years. In January 1981, sixteen Salvadoreans were deported for having participated in a demonstration organized by Costa Ricans in support of El Salvador. The refugees were arrested, beaten, and kept without food (*Derechos Humanos en Centroamérica* 1981, 9).

In April 1981 the *Universidad Semanal* (a newspaper published at the University of Costa Rica) reported that the Judicial Investigation Body (OIJ) and the Office of Prevention of Delinquency (UPD), together with the Immigration Office, concentrated their efforts on locating, detaining, and deporting foreigners under the pretext of doing away with "masked tourism." Their strategy involved breaking into houses, searching for arms and "subversive" literature, and threatening people with deportation. At that time, fifty to one hundred people, especially Salvadoreans, were deported each month. Some victims of arrest complained that the immigration officers had first taken away their documents and then had arrested them for not having documents. In some cases, books and magazines characterized as subversive by immigration officers became a sufficient cause for deportation (*Universidad Semanal*, April 1982, 12–13).

Finally, in 1983, the Costa Rican government introduced strict visa control for Salvadorean tourists. This measure virtually put an end to the Salvadorean refugee flow. Costa Rica did not close its doors to all refugees, however. Starting in 1983, Nicaraguans began pouring into the country. By 1986 there were 30,000 refugees officially recognized and, according to some estimates, as many as 250,000 undocumented Nicaraguans dispersed throughout the country (*La Nación*, 22 September 1986). The contrast between restrictive policies towards Salvadorean refugees and acceptance of Nicaraguan refugees can be explained as a response to economic conditions prevailing in the country, to the perception of national security threats, and, most importantly, to foreign policy interests.[2]

ECONOMIC CONDITIONS

After its victory in 1948, the National Liberation party introduced a number of reforms that included three major objectives: diversification of agricultural exports, development of national industry, and expansion of the state (Rojas 1984, 136). These reforms resulted in steady economic growth in Costa Rica between 1950 and the mid 1970s. Then, some signs of "structural imbalances" (Vega 1986) began to appear and culminated in a crisis in the early 1980s. Rovira (1985) summarizes six symptoms of the economic crisis in Costa Rica:

• In 1981 the GDP decreased by 2 per cent and in 1982 by 7 per cent.

- Open unemployment stood at 8.7 per cent in 1981 and climbed to 9.4 per cent in 1982.
- The inflation rate rose to 65 per cent in 1981 and to more than 80 per cent in 1982.
- The foreign exchange rate went from 8.6 to 60 colones to the U.S. dollar between 1980 and 1982.
- The average real wage decreased from 1441 colones (US$165) to 858 colones (US$100) per month between March 1979 and November 1982.
- The external debt increased from US$1870 million to US$3497 million between 1978 and 1982. Most of the latter (US$2860 million) was composed of the public debt.

The government decided to restrict entry of Salvadorean refugees at the time when the economic crisis in Costa Rica reached its peak. It was more difficult to control the refugee flow from Nicaragua, which is separated from Costa Rica by a poorly patrolled 220-mile border that passes through the jungle along the San Juan River.

As the economic crisis escalated in 1983, the International Monetary Fund refused to renegotiate the Costa Rican debt unless it introduced an austerity program. While fearing negative political repercussions, the Costa Rican government did introduce stabilization policies that included a state monopoly over foreign exchange, increased taxes, and extension of credit to the private sector. These measures were approved by the Reagan administration, which subsequently increased aid to the country dramatically. As a result, the Costa Rican economy started to show signs of recovery: the GDP grew by 2.3 per cent in 1983 and by 6.6 per cent in 1984; open unemployment dropped from 9.4 per cent to 7 per cent between 1982 and 1984; the inflation rate also dropped, from 80 per cent to 10.7 per cent between 1982 and 1983; the foreign exchange rate improved from 70 to 48 colones to the U.S. dollar between 1982 and 1984; and the real average monthly wage rose from 858 to 1268 colones between 1982 and 1984 (Rovira 1985, 36).

These improvements were merely superficial, since the introduced policies failed to address structural problems that had led to the crisis. On the surface, however, it seemed that the economic conditions were improving and, at least in the early years, it appeared that the economic burden the Nicaraguan refugees would impose on Costa Rica were not of major concern.[3]

PERCEIVED SECURITY THREAT

The determination of refugee status in Costa Rica has always been intimately linked to national security concerns. In 1980 President Rodrigo Carazo announced that the Ministry of Public Security was responsible for determining and documenting refugees. In 1982 President Luis Alberto Monge placed immigration under the control of the newly formed National Security Council (Ambos 1987, 6–7). Official policies towards refugees have been strongly coloured by whether they were perceived to pose a threat to national security. Salvadorean refugees were often seen as guerrilla supporters and therefore as a security threat to Costa Rica. The Los Angeles project serves as an illustration.

The Los Angeles farm, located in the province of Liberia, was the biggest rural refugee settlement project in Costa Rica. Because a considerable number of Salvadorean refugees were settled on the farm (at one point more than a thousand), it became an object of concern for those who viewed refugees as subversives.

On 7 February 1981, thirty rural policemen entered the farm early in the morning to search for arms and "subversive" documents (*La Nación*, 30 September 1983). On 3 October 1982 an article entitled "Guerrilla School in Liberia" was published in *La República*. This article quoted the report submitted by the State Security Council which stated that refugees living in Los Angeles were being trained as guerrillas to be sent back to El Salvador. The report also suggested that some communist activists were trying to recruit refugees to join the guerrillas, and that some arms were hidden in Los Angeles. On 5 October 1982 *La Nación* published the list of the major "organizers" and "indoctrinators" operating in the camp. The next day, six Salvadorean schoolteachers from Los Angeles were arrested by immigration officials. They were detained and threatened with deportation (*La Nación*, 9 October 1982).

Refugee groups and human rights committees made public protests against the allegations. They were especially indignant about the publication of the list of the supposed political activists operating in the camp, since this list put the lives of their relatives still in El Salvador in danger. In response to their protests, *Costa Rica Libre*, an extreme right-wing organization, responded with an article (*La Nación*, 25 October 1982) that, among other things, stated: "Apart from engaging themselves in activities which are publicly denounced as dangerous for national security, Marxist foreigners allow themselves the luxury of criticising and insulting government authorities … Not being satisfied with the scandal, they now criticise the Costa Rican government on its own territory. This is simply incredible."

The view that Salvadorean refugees spread political violence is often expressed in Costa Rica's major newspapers. On 7 October 1982 an article published in *La República* reported that government officials were alarmed by the massive arrival of Salvadorean refugees (a figure of 15,000 people was cited). It was said that "the country, virtually without realising it, may have served as training grounds for extremists who then return to El Salvador as well trained guerrillas." No proof of guerrilla activities on Costa Rican territory was ever presented.

By contrast, many Nicaraguan contras were found not only at the border with Nicaragua but in refugee camps as well (Ambos 1987, 54–5; Loescher 1988, 316). Nevertheless, no allegations of subversive activities have been brought against Nicaraguan refugees by Costa Rican officials. This difference in perception of the threat to internal security can be attributed to concerns about Costa Rican foreign policy.

FOREIGN POLICY INTERESTS

Costa Rica started to receive massive movements of refugees in the late 1970s under the presidency of Rodrigo Carazo. Carazo hoped to present Costa Rica as the "Switzerland of Central America," and he established the judicial and institutional structures for dealing with refugees. He perceived the refugee problem to be of state importance, and he appointed the Office of the Presidency to preside over the National Commission for Refugees formed in 1980. With the exception of three years between 1982 and 1985 when refugee affairs were moved to the Ministry of Justice, the Presidency has always been the major decision maker on refugee matters (Ambos 1987). The fact that the Ministry of the Exterior has been a member of the commission since 1980 (Ambos 1987) illustrates that external relations have been an important element in formulating refugee policy.

At the beginning of the 1980s as Central American politics were polarizing, Costa Rica formed a united block with El Salvador, Honduras, and Guatemala against Nicaragua. In October 1982 President Monge announced a policy of neutrality or nonalignment towards any political group or nation in conflict with other Central American countries. Yet from the beginning of his term as president, Monge indicated a shift in policy towards closer alignment with the United States in opposition to the Sandinista government. In October 1982 Foreign Minister Fernando Volio Jimenez set up a Forum for Peace and Democracy that originally excluded both Nicaragua and Guatemala (Ferris 1987, 70). Later, Guatemala was invited to join the group. In 1985 Monge explicitly approved Reagan's efforts to obtain more support from the U.S. Congress for contra aid (*Costa Rica: Balance de la Situación,* no. 10, October 1984–May 1985). Even though Monge did try to maintain independence from the Reagan administration and at times criticized U.S. policies (Blachman and Hellman 1986, 175–6), the country's economic vulnerability and its dependence on economic and military aid from the United States (Blachman and Hellman 1986, 168–79; Fagen 1987, 140) made it very difficult for Monge to disagree with Reagan's views on the region's politics.[4] During his term, Monge constantly attacked Nicaragua for being a totalitarian dictatorship (Ferris 1987, 70). The massive exodus of refugees from Nicaragua was publicly manipulated to prove to the international community that the Sandinista government was repressive, and the refugees were warmly received.

By contrast, it was not in the interests of Costa Rican foreign policy to grant asylum to Salvadorean refugees. Indirectly, this would have meant accusing El Salvador of violating human rights. By deporting Salvadorean refugees and thus failing to offer protection to them, the Costa Rican government was turning a blind eye to political repression in El Salvador. By closing doors to Salvadorean refugees in 1983, the Costa Rican government made a statement that it recognized improvements with respect to human rights in their country. In comparison with previous years, violence in El Salvador had decreased and violations of human rights had become more selective, although they were still widespread.

PUBLIC ATTITUDES

Middle and upper-class Costa Ricans held negative views of Salvadoreans, corresponding to those presented in the conservative mass
media (see chapter 3). Most poorer Costa Ricans, however, gave them
a warm reception. In fact, many Costa Ricans (at least those with
whom I discussed the subject) believe that Salvadoreans, unlike
Nicaraguans, are hard workers. The long history of hostile relations
between Costa Rica and Nicaragua (Ferris 1987, 68) produced a
backlash against Nicaraguan refugees (*La Prensa Libre*, 10 May
1983; *La Nación*, 22 September 1986; *La Prensa Libre*, 10 November
1986). So much hostility was directed towards Nicaraguans that, by
comparison, Salvadoreans were generally viewed in favourable terms.
Thus, restrictive official policies towards Salvadorean (as opposed to
Nicaraguan) refugees did not reflect public attitudes towards them.

LABOUR LAWS FOR REFUGEES

Prior to 1980, refugees recognized by UNHCR had been subject to
labour legislation for foreigners in general, which allowed them to
work as long as they did not replace national labour. In 1980, when
refugees were granted legal acceptance, their participation in the
labour market was limited to the so-called durable solution projects.
A UNHCR memorandum stated: "It is worth clarifying that a refugee
as a general rule does not have a right to work in Costa Rica. They
can only be authorised to work in self-administered businesses
financed by the UNHCR ... The National Immigration Council is a
body responsible for the approval of job authorisations for refugees
participating in such businesses."

These restrictive labour laws could be justified in the light of the
economic crisis faced by Costa Rica at the time. The primary objective of the Costa Rican government was to protect national labour
from competition. Therefore, refugees were allowed to work only in
those jobs specifically created for them.

In 1984, as the Costa Rican economy started showing signs of
recovery, the Costa Rican government reconsidered its labour policy
towards refugees. Under pressure from UNHCR, the government
issued a new law in September 1984 that allowed refugees to work
as wage laboureres. This new law stated:

Refugees recognised by the present decree will enjoy the right to work in the national territory. These permits will be authorised by the Refugee Office [of the National Immigration Council] in coordination with the respective functionary of the Ministry of Labour, who will take into consideration the condition of non-displacement of national labour, in conjunction with such factors as a specific economic activity, geographic location and criteria and policies dictated by CONAPARE (Campos 1985, 83).

The permits were in agreement with the Costa Rican labour code, which stated that at least 90 per cent of a firm's workers had to be Costa Ricans, and that they had to receive at least 85 per cent of total salaries (*Estudio Sobre la Situación Jurídica de Asilados, Refugiados y Personas Desplazadas* 1983, 69).

In August 1985 a Mixed Committee made up of representatives from the Ministry of Labour, the President's Office, the Ministry of Justice, and the Public Security Office was authorized to issue job permits to refugees. CONAPARE was renamed DIGEPARE (General Directorate for Refugees), and it was moved from the Ministry of Justice to the President's Office. Danilo Jimenez, the minister of the President's Office, explained in his interview with the *Universidad Semanal* that the change was dictated by the importance of the problem. He contended: "The life of refugees will be dignified through their participation in productive activities so that they will not have to live, without dignity, off international charity, but instead will be able to produce for themselves and for the country." He suggested that it was Costa Rica's duty, as a democratic country, to protect refugees and to make them productive. He added that it was important to fight against the xenophobia so common among Costa Ricans (*Universidad Semanal*, August–September 1985, 24–5).

NATURALIZATION

The legal constraints on the refugees' right to work applied as long as they maintained refugee status. Another alternative available to refugees was to become residents and naturalized citizens. One year after having obtained residency, foreign residents could apply for naturalization, provided they were over twenty-one years of age, did not have a criminal record, and were willing to renounce their previous citizenship (*Estudio Sobre la Situación Jurídica de Asilados, Refugiados y Personas Desplazadas* 1983, 84–5).

In June 1986 it was reported that about eighty Central Americans were becoming naturalized citizens each week. Nicaraguans and Salvadoreans constituted 80 per cent of the total (*Nación*, 25 July 1986).

While immigration authorities felt it was too easy to become a Costa Rican citizen, most refugees I interviewed complained it was too difficult to become even a resident. The major difficulty was economic, since in 1986 a refugee had to deposit 12,000 colones (US$230) and pay 3000 colones (US$58) annually, in addition to lawyers' fees (approximately 15,000 colones or US$290), to obtain this status. Moreover, the procedure took too long. In 1986, for instance, I met a Salvadorean man, married to a Costa Rican woman, father of a three-year-old girl born in Costa Rica, employed in a Costa Rican firm, who was still waiting for the results of his application made in 1985.

The obligation to renounce their Salvadorean citizenship also discouraged some refugees from applying for naturalization, because they were still hoping to return to El Salvador one day. Some Salvadoreans were hesitant about applying for residency because they automatically lost their refugee status and certain privileges this status afforded them, such as paid medical insurance, the possibility of migrating to a third country, and some assistance programs. Although I could not obtain any exact figures, I would estimate that most of the sixty-four (80 per cent of eighty) Central Americans who became citizens each month were not refugees but better-off economic immigrants.

3   Social Integration of Salvadoreans

In many respects Salvadoreans resemble Costa Ricans. They speak the same language, even though their dialects are different. There are somatic similarities between them, and their cultural beliefs and behaviour are more similar than different. Negative stereotypes of Salvadoreans that exist among the urban middle and upper classes in Costa Rica do not prevent a relatively smooth interaction between Salvadoreans and Costa Ricans who find themselves in similar economic circumstances. Because the urban informal sector[1] has not become saturated in Costa Rica, there does not seem to be a competition between Salvadorean and national small-scale producers; hence the two groups are not hostile towards each other. At the same time, the Salvadorean community is not isolated. While Salvadoreans tried to organize social, political, and cultural activities in the first few years after they came to Costa Rica, by 1986 very few such functions took place. Most Salvadoreans interacted with Costa Ricans on the daily basis, and most of the time this interaction was peaceful.

DIFFERENCES BETWEEN SALVADOREANS AND COSTA RICANS

Salvadoreans can be distinguished from Costa Ricans (*Ticos*) in two ways: physiognomy and language. Costa Rica has a large white population (*blancos*), either direct descendants of Spanish colonizers

Table 3
Differences in Costa Rican and Salvadorean Vocabulary

Costa Rican	Salvadorean	English translation
güila	cipote	child
vainica	ejote	green bean
chivilla	rápida	mini-bus
pulpería	tienda	small food store
gallo pinto	casamiento	fried rice and beans
limon dulce	lima	sweet lemon
faja	cincho	belt
perro	chucho	dog
tuanis	vergon	OK (slang)

or with minimal Indian blood. Most Salvadorean people, in contrast, are *morenos* (swarthy) or *mestizos* (mixed). Some of them have distinct Indian facial characteristics (*cara india*), such as black round eyes and straight black hair. Others have a swarthy complexion. This identifies them as not Costa Rican, although not necessarily Salvadorean, since their facial features resemble those of Nicaraguans, Guatemalans, or Peruvians, for instance.

These images are to a large extent stereotypical, however, since there are many exceptions to this "ideal type" distinction. Many *blancos* Salvadoreans come from Chalatenango, a province in El Salvador that became a conflict zone at the beginning of the civil war and produced a considerable number of refugees, many of whom came to Costa Rica. And many *Guanacastecos* from the northern Costa Rican province of Guanacaste, are *morenos* and resemble a "typical" Salvadorean.

Salvadoreans and Costa Ricans also speak a different Spanish dialect. Some examples of differences in vocabulary between the two countries are presented in table 3. The linguistic differences between the two cultures lie not only in vocabulary but also in grammatical constructions and in pronunciation. For instance, where a Costa Rican would use the simple past of the verb *ir* (to go), a Salvadorean would use the past principle (*fue* and *ha ido*, respectively). Salvadoreans pronounce *ll* and *y* in words like *silla*, *llegar*, and *yo* as *j*, while Costa Ricans pronounce them as *ie*. Whereas Salvadoreans roll the *r*, Costa Ricans pronounce it in a softer way, resembling the English pronunciation of this letter, especially at the end of words and when *r* is preceded by *t*.

These linguistic differences are obvious to a newly arrived Salvadorean in Costa Rica. After a few years of living in the country, however, the differences become blurred, especially in vocabulary. When talking to Costa Ricans, Salvadoreans adopt the vocabulary that will be readily understood. Eventually they adopt these words in their own vocabulary. Sometimes, when talking to another Salvadorean, they use a "Costa Rican" word and add, "as Costa Ricans would say it." Although most Salvadoreans make fun of the Costa Rican pronunciation and insist on pronouncing words in the "Salvadorean" style, they realize the extent to which their accent has changed when they come to a third country of resettlement (such as Canada) and talk to other Salvadoreans. This change is more significant among the younger population. The extent to which a Salvadorean changes her or his accent differs from one person to another and ranges between complete "costaricanization" (in the case of a few people) to absolute maintenance of the Salvadorean way of speech, with most people being somewhere in the middle.

When I asked some Salvadoreans to define the difference between themselves and the *Ticos*, they mentioned the following behavioural patterns. While Costa Ricans eat mainly bread or industrially produced small and thin tortillas, Salvadoreans like thick, home-made tortillas. Whereas in El Salvador they grind maize flower, in Costa Rica they buy ready-made, milled flour. They do, however, make tortillas by hand, whereas *Ticos*, even when they make tortillas at home, use a press. According to a Salvadorean informant, Costa Ricans call Salvadoreans *maiceros* (maize eaters) because of their pattern of tortilla consumption. A traditional Salvadorean dish is *pupusas*, stuffed tortillas. Many Salvadorean families in Costa Rica eat them at least once a week.

A stronger tradition of machismo is another feature said to distinguish Salvadoreans from Costa Ricans. The Salvadorean family is more male dominated. Women are more submissive and less demanding. It was often mentioned that, unlike Salvadoreans, Costa Rican women like dressing well, use makeup and paint their nails. Costa Rican women go out by themselves at night, whereas Salvadorean women usually go out with an escort. In general, Costa Rican women are believed to be more independent.

The third area where the two cultures are thought to be different is in respect for folk traditions. Whereas Salvadoreans like decorating their houses with handicrafts, wear traditional clothes, and sing *rancheras* or traditional peasant songs, Costa Ricans are usually portrayed by Salvadorean informants as devoid of cultural roots and as imitators of the European and North American contemporary cultures.

The last and most significant difference between the two cultures is thought to be in political ideology. Most Salvadorean refugees are victims of persecution (direct or indirect) by the military forces of the right-wing government. This experience made them, if they were not already, left-wing sympathizers. An average Costa Rican, in contrast, is conservative. Costa Ricans believe that guerrillas, and not the repressive government, are responsible for political unrest in El Salvador, a view reinforced by the conservative mass media; all three major newspapers in Costa Rica, *La Nación, La Prensa Libre*, and *La República*, are controlled by the right wing. Once again, however, these distinctions are stereotypical: there are apolitical Salvadoreans, just as there are leftist Costa Ricans. Although not strong, the Communist party does exist in Costa Rica. Many Costa Ricans, along with Salvadoreans, belonged to solidarity committees in the early 1980s. Poorer Costa Ricans are closer ideologically to Salvadoreans, with whom they share an understanding of exploitation and injustice.

RELATIONS BETWEEN SALVADOREANS
AND COSTA RICANS

Many Costa Ricans view Salvadoreans as illiterate peasants. These stereotypes are held predominantly by urban middle- and upper-class Costa Ricans for whom anyone with a darker complexion, whether national or foreign, is associated with being uneducated and uncultured. Racism towards indigenous people exists throughout Latin America (Bollinger and Lund 1982; Diaz-Polanco 1982; Ortiz 1984; Moody 1988). In Costa Rica it is especially strong because most of the population are of European descent with little, if any, Indian blood. Most of the Salvadorean indigenous population has been exterminated (especially after the 1932 rebellion) or assimilated, and thus made almost "invisible" (Chapin 1989). On the average, however, Salvadoreans are of darker complexion than Costa Ricans.

Approximately half the Salvadoreans in Costa Rican come from rural areas (Vega 1984). Those of rural origin are also victims of prejudice because of the anti-rural bias predominant throughout urban

Latin America (Lipton 1977). This sentiment is relatively strong in Costa Rica, which has a high level of urbanization.

Furthermore, Costa Rica's socialized health care, progressive labour code, social welfare, and absence of an army distinguish it from other Central American countries. According to the 1982 World Development Report, in 1977 the adult literacy rate in El Salvador was 62 per cent while in Costa Rica it was as high as 90 per cent. In 1980, the infant mortality rate for children under one year of age was 78 per cent for El Salvador and 24 per cent for Costa Rica. Most *Ticos* are proud of their country, and often feel superior to other Central Americans.

On occasion, prejudices held by Costa Ricans translate into pejorative remarks directed at Salvadoreans. Several informants reported having been told to go back to El Salvador by Costa Ricans. On one occasion, when I was having lunch in a Salvadorean *soda* (small restaurant), a customer complained about the abundance of flies there and commented that they must have come from El Salvador.

These feelings are much more pronounced on the part of middle- and upper-class urban Costa Ricans. Lower-class *Ticos*, themselves victims of prejudice by those above them on the economic ladder, seem to get along well with Salvadoreans. Several informants reported cases in which Costa Ricans were exceptionally kind to them, offering them food and shelter. Many Salvadoreans belong to Costa Rican religious communities or solidarity committees. Most informants reported no problems in interpersonal relations with Costa Ricans in their neighbourhood or at school and admitted having as many Costa Rican as Salvadorean friends. The rate of intermarriage was also relatively high in Costa Rica. In the eighty-one projects on which I compiled information on marriage, there were thirteen inter- marriages. Many Salvadorean young men preferred going out with Costa Rican women. This was especially true of the more educated males who believed that, in comparison with Costa Rican women, Salvadorean females were more close-minded and therefore less inter- esting. The differences between the two communities, then, did not prevent them from interacting smoothly.

In terms of economic competition between Salvadoreans and Costa Ricans, I do not have sufficient information about those employed in agriculture to make a firm judgment, though several refugee agency workers told me that relations between Salvadoreans in rural projects and national farmers were generally smooth. I can, however, present an analysis of the urban informal sector where many Salvadoreans are employed. Comparative data for Salvadorean urban businesses come out my interviews with members of seventy-five small enterprises.

UNEMPLOYMENT AND GROWTH IN THE INFORMAL ECONOMY IN COSTA RICA

Between 1950 and 1980 all Central American countries experienced rapid urbanization accompanied by an expansion of the modern industrial sector. Employment in the modern sector grew by approximately 4.4 per cent annually in these years (PREALC 1986, 105). The policy of import-substituting industrialization, adopted by the Costa Rican government in the late 1950s, had certain negative effects on small producers. First, industrial enterprises producing textiles, clothes, and shoes posed strong competition to small producers of the same products. The large firms could offer lower prices and better quality products because of their more sophisticated level of technology. Second, small enterprises faced a serious problem in procuring imported raw materials because of the shortage of foreign currency, which was directed towards subsidizing the industrial sector. Third, through advanced advertising techniques, modern industries influenced demand towards the consumption of their products. As a result, during the 1960s and 1970s the proportion of artisanal producers in the total labour force employed in manufacture declined (PREALC 1986, 107). Between 1958 and 1980 big industrial enterprises (defined as those employing more than thirty workers) came to occupy a more significant role. Their percentage in all industrial enterprises rose from 3 per cent to 11 per cent, and the percentage of workers they employed of all industrially employed workers increased from 15 per cent to 55 per cent (Moller 1985a, 4).

Between 1973 and 1976 the level of employment in Costa Rica had a satisfactory growth. While the economically active population grew at a rate of 4 per cent, employment grew at a rate of 4.5 per cent. Beginning in 1976, however, rates of employment started lagging behind the growth of the economically active population. By 1982 it had become a serious problem. Between 1980 and 1982, while the economically active population grew at a rate of 4.4 per cent, employment grew at only 1.7 per cent. About two-thirds of the Costa Rican population faced employment-related problems in 1982 (MIDEPLAN 1983b).

The cost of the basic food basket grew by 357 per cent between 1977 and 1982, whereas the average monthly salary grew by only 122 per cent. In June 1982 the cost of the basic food basket for a family of six was 3367 colones, whereas an average monthly salary was 2957 colones or 14 per cent less (MIDEPLAN 1983a, 17–18). Real wages declined by 30 per cent between 1979 and 1982. The average industrial real wage fell by 38 per cent in this period (PREALC 1985, 5). Declining real wages of workers produced pressure on their family members to join the labour force, mainly in the informal sector and in traditional agriculture.

Almost 40 per cent of nonheads of households worked in small establishments in 1982, compared with only 32 per cent in 1979 (PREALC 1985, 20). They established small businesses mainly in the tertiary sector. The tertiary occupations included small commerce and domestic services, which require limited capital investment, as well as repair of cars, bicycles, radios, television sets, and domestic appliances. The need for these latter services emerged as Central American countries increased imports of these products (PREALC 1986, 105–8). As a whole, the informal sector grew at an annual rate of 4.4 per cent during that period. Yet, in comparison with other Central American countries (with the exception of Panama), the informal sector was not large in Costa Rica (see table 4).

The occupational composition of the national and the Salvadorean urban informal sector in Costa Rica differed one from the other (see table 5). While there was a definite predominance of retail business among Costa Rican informal enterprises, the most significant occupational groups among Salvadoreans were in the textile industry (*costura* and *sastrería*), in food production, such as small restaurants (*soda* and *pupusería*) and bakeries (*panadería*), and in leather production, mainly shoe production and repair workshops (*zapatería*). Because agencies administering and financing projects for refugees chose to assist bakeries and workshops producing clothes and shoes primarily, these enterprises predominated among Salvadoreans. Costa Rican informal enterprises, in contrast, emerged on their own. It is easier to start a small retail business (it requires smaller initial investments), and more than half of the Costa Rican small enterprise

Table 4
Employment in the Informal Sector in Capitals of Central American Countries, 1982

Capital	Total employed population (000s)	Population employed in informal sector (000s)	Percentage employed in informal sector
San José	219.5	51.2	23
San Salvador	313.5	118.8	38
Guatemala City	323.8	97.8	30
Tegucigalpa	148.9	42.9	29
Managua	203.2	71.6	35
Panama	239.7	33.2	14

Source: PREALC (1986), based on Costa Rica: Dirección de Estadística y Censos, tabulaciones especiales de la Encuesta de Hogares, July 1982; El Salvador: Ministerio de Planificación, Encuesta de Hogares de Propósitos Múltiples, 1980; Guatemala: Ministerio de Economía, tabulaciones de la Encuesta Nacional de Gastos e Ingresos; Honduras: Encuesta Especial, April 1982; Nicaragua: Encuesta de Hogares Urbanas, 1982; Panama: Dirección de Estadística y Censos, tabulaciones especiales de la Encuesta de Hogares, July 1982.

Table 5
Occupational Composition for Costa Rican and Salvadorean Enterprise Owners, 1982

Occupational sector	Costa Rican[a]	Salvadorean[b]
	(per cent)	
Retail business	50.1	4.0
Textiles	12.1	28.0
Repairs	8.8	8.0
Leather/wood	8.0	18.7
Personal services	8.0	6.7
Food production	4.5	24.0
Metallic/electric	3.4	0
Crafts	0	6.7
Other	0	4.0
Total	100.0	100.0

a Ministerio de Trabajo y Seguridad (1983), based on the Encuesta de Establecimientos Pequeños, compiled by the Ministry of Labour and Security, projected into 1982 by General Directorate of Statistics and Census and the General Directorate of Labour Planning.
b Survey of seventy-five Salvadorean enterprises.
Note: This study used three criteria to define informal enterprises: first, enterprises were to employ no more than five wage-labourers; second, professional enterprises owners were excluded; third, domestic service was excluded.

owners were in this occupational category. Since the occupational composition of the Costa Rican and the Salvadorean informal sectors was different, most of them were not in direct competition.

Table 6
Type of Clientele for Costa Rican and Salvadorean Enterprise Owners

Clients	Costa Rican[a]	Salvadorean[a]
	(per cent)	
Private customers	82.1	61.3
Stores	14.3	26.7
Factory	2.3	5.3
Other	1.3	6.7

a Ministry of Labour and Security (1983)
b Survey of seventy-five Salvadorean enterprises

Because many Costa Rican small enterprise owners were engaged in small commerce, they relied heavily on private customers. Salvadorean small producers sold less to individuals and more to stores than did the Costa Ricans (see table 6).

Salvadorean small urban enterprises did not have a significant advantage over Costa Rican enterprises in their access to institutional assistance. Costa Rican small urban producers also enjoyed some institutional assistance. For instance, the Department of Small Industry and Crafts of the Ministry of Industry, Energy, and Mines set up the Urban Development program (PDU), with funds provided by USAID. The aim was to assist small enterprises with fewer than twenty workers with fixed capital not exceeding US$10,000 – US$15,000. In the four years this program existed, 2291 small businesses received loans (Haans 1985, 84).

In December 1982 the Ministry of Labour and Social Security signed an agreement with the Popular Bank of Community Development to allocate 70 million colones for the creation of small individual and cooperative projects. About 3200 people (mainly in agriculture) benefited from this program in 1982 and 1983 (*Ministerio de Trabajo y Seguridad* 1986). There were many more agencies assisting small Costa Rican enterprises, in the form of loans, training, and technical assistance, in the 1980s (see Moller 1985a).

Not every Costa Rican small enterprise, enjoyed access to aid nor did the Salvadoreans who received assistance form a petty bourgeoisie within the Costa Rican informal sector. Comparison of Costa Rican and Salvadorean small producers showed that the two groups had much in common. They earned comparable incomes and faced similar problems related to production. In fact, according to some

Table 7
Monthly Income Levels for Costa Rican and Salvadorean Enterprise Owners

Income levels	Costa Rican[a]	Salvadorean[b]
	(per cent)	
Less than minimum wage	34	60 (55)[c]
Minimum wage–double minimum wage	33	20 (30)[c]
Double minimum wage	33	20 (15)[c]

a Moller (1985b)
b Survey of seventy-five Salvadorean enterprises
c The second figure is based on calculations of the adjusted income.
Note: Minimum monthly wage is taken to be 2145 colones in Moller's study for 1982 data, whereas in 1986 it was 6637 colones.

reports, Costa Rican small producers did better economically than the Salvadoreans under study.

One-third of small enterprise owners analysed by Moller (1985b) were found to earn less than the minimum wage. Another third, however, were earning double the minimum wage. In Moller's analysis, incomes of those employed in the informal sector are relatively high, possibly because he includes enterprises hiring up to fourteen people. Haans (1985), who defines informal enterprises as hiring no more than five wage-labourers, reported that about 25 per cent of those working in small enterprises had difficulties satisfying their basic needs in 1982. About one-half of these people lived in extreme poverty. (It should be remembered, however, that in 1982 Costa Rica was at the peak of its economic crisis.) Incomes of Salvadorean enterprise owners are even lower than those reported by Moller for Costa Ricans (see table 7).

In sum, in comparison with other countries, the Costa Rican informal sector was far from being saturated in the 1980s. It was composed predominantly of pedlars, while institutions assisting Salvadoreans promoted mainly bakeries and workshops making clothing and shoes. By catering to a different clientele or to the same clientele but offering a different product, Salvadoreans were not often in competition with national small producers and vendors. Costa Rican small producers also received some financial aid and were not disadvantaged in relation to the assisted Salvadoreans. A comparison of their incomes shows that, in fact, Salvadoreans were not better off than Costa Ricans. In other words, they did not seem to pose a threat to the national labour force in the informal sector.

COMMUNITY RESOURCES

How well are Salvadoreans organized in Costa Rica? Is the Salvadorean community, to use Breton's (1964, 1978) phrase, "institutionally complete"? Does it have enough ethnic resources to allow it to make only minimal contact with members of other ethnic groups?

In 1986 most Salvadorean students attended Costa Rican academic and vocational schools and universities. One school, run by Salvadorean teachers, offered literacy classes to adults and some help to students who were behind in their studies in regular schools, as well as a course in embroidery. There were also two day care centres for Salvadorean refugee children. These three educational institutions, all located in Heredia, served a total of about one hundred children and adults.

In terms of the media, one newsletter was published by the *Coordinadora* (an organization coordinating Salvadorean refugees in Costa Rica), another by the young Christian movement, and occasional leaflets were produced by various political movements. These papers circulated mainly among members of these organizations. Most refugees relied on Costa Rican newspapers as the major source of information.

Like Costa Ricans, most Salvadoreans are Catholic. In the early 1970s, however, a new type of Catholic religious movement known as liberation theology emerged in El Salvador and led to the creation of the "popular church" (*iglesia popular*). Liberation theology challenged traditional views held by the Catholic church on the preservation of the status quo, and approved an armed political struggle for justice. This religious movement was widespread in rural areas of El Salvador that later became conflict zones.

One of the preachers of liberation theology, Padre Inocente (a pseudonym), who was persecuted in El Salvador, fled to Costa Rica and established a popular church in the Fatima Refuge. Other Salvadorean and Costa Rican priests also formed religious communities where popular masses were celebrated. In the early 1980s a large number of people were involved in these religious communities. By 1985, when I joined them, they had become considerably smaller. Padre Inocente's Sunday masses usually brought together about forty worshippers. These religious services not only had religious significance but also served to strengthen the ethnic identity of the participants. During the masses, such themes as the political situation of El Salvador, Salvadorean religious martyrs, problems of adaptation to Costa Rican life, and other topics relevant to the life of Salvadoreans in Costa Rica were discussed. They also promoted a sense of pride in being a Salvadorean and in being a refugee. During one of the celebrations, Padre Inocente stated: "The voice of refugees is a prophetic voice." Although very few participated in these religious activities on a regular basis, special celebrations organized by various Salvadorean religious communities attracted up to 150 worshippers. These events included the International Day of the Saviour, the patron of El Salvador, and the commemoration of the death of Monsignor Romero.

Apart from political parties, to which unfortunately I had no access, there were two Salvadorean cultural organizations, five theatre groups, and five music bands active in Costa Rica in the summer of 1985. The most important Salvadorean cultural organization was the Instituto Cultural Costarricense-Salvadoreño (Costa Rican–Salvadorean Cultural Institute). The objective of this organization was to promote cultural exchange between Costa Ricans and Salvadoreans. This took place through concerts that expressed the political unity shared by Salvadoreans and progressive Costa Ricans (as well as immigrants/refugees from other countries, such as Argentina or Chile). Salvadorean refugees were given free tickets to attend these functions every Monday (*Lunes Cultural*). During the summer of 1985, several Salvadorean music and theatre groups gave presentations at the Instituto.

In the seven months of 1986, however, most of the "exchange" was rather one-sided. Only Costa Rican (or other non-Salvadorean) musicians and actors were invited to perform. The problem was that by 1986 all Salvadorean music and theatre groups, except for one, had disbanded. Most of the members of these groups were young people who used to study while they received UNHCR emergency aid. When this aid was discontinued in 1985, they had to join the labour force and had no time to engage in cultural activities. Another reason these groups disappeared was the migration of some of their members to third countries. Some Salvadorean musicians joined a Peruvian band, Proyección Andina (Andean Projection), because Andean music was more acceptable to Costa Ricans and therefore allowed musicians some financial rewards. Other Salvadoreans were in the process of forming a band in 1986. About one-half of the band's members were Costa Ricans. The same was true of a pantomime group that had survived but retained only two of its original members, supplementing them with a Polish, a Ukrainian, and several Costa Rican performers. This composition had a definite impact on the content of its presentations, which included considerably less Salvadorean and more international and Costa Rican themes.

Only a small network of Salvadoreans participated in activities at the Instituto in 1986. While in 1985 Salvadorean refugees were given free tickets, in 1986 Salvadoreans had to pay for some of the activities of the Instituto. When the Instituto called a meeting in October 1986 to form a committee to raise funds for victims of the earthquake in El Salvador, most of the people who attended were non-Salvadoreans. This turnout could only be partially explained by the weak political base among Salvadoreans in Costa Rica. The inability of the Instituto to communicate information to a wider network of Salvadorean refugees was also a factor. Even a week after the quake, only about eighty Salvadoreans attended the benefit concert at the Instituto for the victims of the earthquake.

The second cultural group, MCS (Salvadorean Cultural Movement) had a low profile in the community and organized few activities. In July 1985 it presented a concert in celebration of the tenth anniversary of the founding of the Salvadorean Students' United Front (Frente Unitario de Estudiantes Salvadoreños). Of all the functions I attended in Costa Rica, this one had the most Salvadorean content. Both the performers and the audience were predominantly Salvadorean. The concert, which started with a presentation of the national anthem of El Salvador, included performances by several Salvadorean music groups, demonstrations of videos about the political life of El Salvador, and presentation of a children's folkdance troupe. One five-year-old boy recited a poem that stated: "I am going back to my country. Please do not try to stop me. I am going to grow maize there." *Pupusas* and Salvadorean handicrafts were sold during the celebration. The concert ended with a discussion of the imminent cessation of the UNHCR emergency aid.

During my seven-month stay in Costa Rica in 1986, MCS organized only one cultural event: a commemoration of the massacre of Salvadorean students. Not a single performer was Salvadorean, though some *pupusas* and Salvadorean handicrafts were sold during the performance. The event was presented at the National University of Costa Rica, and most of the audience was Costa Rican.

Another cultural organization, known as Casa de la Cultura (House of Culture), existed for a year between 1982 and 1983 and ran literary, drama, and handicrafts workshops for Salvadorean refugees. In 1983 it closed because of a shortage of funds.

Apart from activities organized by these religious and cultural institutions, occasional dances were part of the social life of Salvadorean refugees. However, they seldom numbered more than four or five a year.

According to Salvadorean informants, community life was considerably richer in the early 1980s. Many activities, including demonstrations, concerts, conferences, and dances, took place and many people participated in them. Salvadoreans identified four reasons why these activities had diminished by 1986. First, after five or six years in exile, many people had lost faith in the imminent victory of the Salvadorean guerrillas and were no longer interested in active participation. Second, Salvadoreans realized that Costa Rica was not as democratic as it was portrayed in the mass media. Left-wing political activities were repressed and Salvadorean activities, whether political or cultural (which of course always had some political implications), were not welcome. The first bitter encounter between Salvadoreans and Costa Rican government officials took place in October 1980, during the commemoration of the death of Salvadorean martyrs, when participants were surrounded by the police and some of them were detained by immigration officers. Having experienced repression once before in their own country, many Salvadoreans were afraid to continue expressing their political opinions publicly. Although a certain degree of political conservatism has always existed in Costa Rica, in 1984–85 relations between the United States and Costa Rica were strengthened, a process of militarization was underway in Costa Rica, relations with Nicaragua were deteriorating, and the more right-wing party, Unidad Demócrata Cristiana (Christian Democratic Unity), was gaining popularity.[2] Consequently, the fear of political repression grew among Salvadorean refugees.

Third, in 1985–86 the Salvadorean community in Costa Rica was *descabezada*, that is, it lacked the leadership necessary to organize for political action. One important community leader died of a heart attack in 1985, and others had left. Costa Rica gave no opportunities for professionals to work in their field, and that led many of them to move to other countries. Furthermore, there were better possibilities for political work in Mexico, the United States, and Canada. The Costa Rican refugee community was very poor and lacked the resources to link itself to the political movement either inside El Salvador or in exile. At the same time, Coordinadora, which was created to be a coordinating body for all Salvadoreans, had a poor reputation and its leaders had been accused of promoting their own interests and appropriating funds given to them by international agencies. Fourth, whereas in 1981 most Salvadorean refugees received UNHCR emergency aid and had free time to engage in social, cultural, and political activities, by 1985 most of them had to work (often more than eight hours a day) to make a living.

The weakness of the Salvadorean community in Costa Rica can also be explained by the political divisions within it. There were five major political movements among the Salvadoreans: MNR (Movimiento Nacional Revolucionario – the National Revolutionary Movement), MPSC (Movimiento Popular Social Cristiana – Popular Social Christian Movement), the Bloque Popular Revolucionario (Revolutionary Popular Bloque), LP 28 (Ligas Populares 28 de Febrero – Popular Leagues of the 28th of February), and MLP (Movimiento de Liberación Popular – Popular Liberation Movement). Sometimes, members of these political movements collaborated; most of the time, however, members of one political movement did not attend functions organized by the other political movements. Members of one music band, for instance, were not allowed to play in it unless they joined the political movement that subsidized it. This requirement led to the splitup of the band.

In 1986 there were several businesses selling Salvadorean products in Costa Rica: four *pupuserías*, one imported clothing store, one workshop producing traditional textiles, two workshops producing handicrafts, and four bakeries making bread. One project that formerly produced Salvadorean leather goods had closed, owing to lack of demand, and the only surviving member preferred to make fine leather briefcases, purses, and wallets. Only two *pupuserías*, one of which formed part of the Instituto, had a predominantly Salvadorean clientele. The Salvadorean textiles and handicrafts were sold mainly to North American tourists or were exported abroad. Three bakers had a mixed, equally divided clientele, and one bakery catered mainly to Costa Rican customers. Salvadorean imported clothes were sold to Costa Rican customers only, possibly because the store was located far from where most Salvadoreans resided.

Most Salvadoreans resided in San José, Heredia, and Alajuela. Within these cities and their surroundings there was no residential segregation of Salvadorean refugees. In 1985 Barrio Jesus was identified by some informants as an area of concentration of Salvadorean families. Some fifteen Salvadorean families lived in this semi-urban, predominantly Costa Rican community, though there was not much unity, social interaction, or economic cooperation among them. By 1986 only half of the families remained. Another area of concentration of Salvadorean refugees was Barrio Bajo de los Molinos. This community was similar to Barrio Jesus. Salvadorean families were dispersed, and interacted no more frequently among themselves than they did with their Costa Rican neighbours.

In sum, Salvadoreans got along with lower-class Costa Ricans well. There were no major differences between them, and neither group felt threatened by the other because the economic competition between them had not become acute. This warm reception on the part of the Costa Rican population was counterbalanced by the legal and economic restrictions that were imposed by government agencies. These restrictions prevented the smooth integration of Salvadoreans into Costa Rican life.

PART TWO
Refugee Aid

4 Settlement of Refugees: Types of Assistance

Refugees require economic aid and health care, psychological treatment, and educational, legal, and other services. The adequacy of a settlement program can be judged on the basis of how well refugee needs are satisfied. In Costa Rica, many agencies participated in the settlement of refugees: some international and some domestic, some governmental and some volunteer. The types of assistance these agencies provided to Salvadorean refugees can be divided into ten areas: relief; education; medical/psychological care; residence; cultural and political work; job permits; legal aid; religious work; food supplements; and development projects. I will outline the first nine briefly, while focusing on employment-creating projects.

RELIEF

Relief assistance to Salvadorean refugees in Costa Rica was provided mainly through the UNHCR emergency assistance program that began in May 1980 and terminated in December 1985. The object of the program was to provide for refugees' basic food and shelter needs. The aid was distributed on the basis of family size. A family of six, for instance, received 2795 colones per month in 1983, and 3775 colones[1] per month in 1985 (see tables 8 and 9). In 1983 a family of six received 1395 colones per month for food, less than one-half of the cost of the basic food basket in Costa Rica that year.[2] In 1985

Table 8
UNHCR Monthly Aid according to Size of Family, 1983

	1	2	3	4	5	6	7
Food	730	810	990	1,125	1,250	1,395	1,575
Rent	350	900	1,100	1,200	1,300	1,400	1,600
Total	1,080	1,710	2,090	2,325	2,550	2,795	3,175

Table 9
UNHCR Monthly Aid according to Size of Family, 1985

	1	2	3	4	5	6	7
Food	1,168	1,423	1,485	1,635	1,750	1,885	1,935
Rent	560	1,395	1,650	1,740	1,820	1,890	1,950
Total	1,728	2,818	3,135	3,375	3,570	3,775	3,885

the discrepancy between UNHCR assistance and the cost of the basic food basket was less evident. The UNHCR increased its assistance for food by 50 per cent between 1983 and 1984, while the inflation rate during that period was 19 per cent.

During the five years, 1980–5, all Salvadoreans who had "convention" refugee status were able to receive assistance under this program, provided they were not assisted by other agencies. Those refugees who were members of urban projects promoted by Caritas lost this assistance. Other urban projects promoted by voluntary agencies that did not have enough funds to pay refugees received UN assistance over the first three to six months of the projects' existence or until self-sufficiency was reached. The same was true in some rural projects. Since most of the rural projects did not reach self-sufficiency within six months, their members continued to receive aid for a longer time.

In 1985 the UNHCR emergency aid program for Salvadorean refugees was discontinued for two reasons. First, the growing Nicaraguan refugee population in Costa Rica put a strain on UNHCR emergency aid funds. Second, both governmental and nongovernmental bodies in charge of refugee settlement felt that the prolonged emergency aid had contributed to the creation of a "dependency syndrome" by refugee assistance workers (Clark 1986). When refugees are forced to rely on external aid, they gradually lose their motivation to work and to provide for themselves. UNHCR decided this program had to be discontinued. The decision created resentment and panic on the part of Salvadorean refugees who had grown to count on it in the absence of real opportunities to find employment.

While relief aid to Salvadorean refugees as a program came to an end in December 1985, UNHCR continued to provide sporadic emergency aid to those in need, particularly to people with disabilities, the elderly, orphans, and single mothers. Thus, in the first six months of 1986, 1837 Salvadoreans (approximately one-third of all Salvadorean refugees) benefited from it. The UNCHR emergency aid was distributed first by PRIMAS (Refugee Program of the Mixed Institute of Social Assistance) and then by CASP/Re (Centre for Social and Political Analysis for Refugees), a nongovernmental agency that replaced it.

In addition to UNHCR, the Episcopalian church and OARS (Office of Orientation and Assistance to Salvadorean Refugees) gave a moderate amount of emergency aid to refugees. The church offered emergency aid to some fifty families (150 people), while OARS made it available to about four hundred people – either single women and men or family heads – per month in 1986.

EDUCATION

Several agencies catered to the educational needs of refugees. PRIMAS, CASP/Re, and Diakonia offered scholarships to grade school and university students. PRIMAS and CASP/Re also ran a project for children with learning difficulties. Coordinadora for Salvadorean Refugees (Coordinadora, for short) offered two literacy courses for about sixty refugees and a course in handicrafts for twenty to thirty women.

The YMCA and CECAMURESA (Training Centre for Salvadorean Refugee Women) provided technical training, the former to young Salvadorean men and the latter to Salvadorean women. In 1981 the YMCA began to offer carpentry, tailoring, electricity, drama, and handicrafts classes taught by Salvadorean teachers, with the hope they could prepare young men for productive projects. In 1982 a decree was passed obliging refugees to receive classes at INA (National Institute for Training) from Costa Rican teachers. As a result the YMCA had to close its own classes. This decree did not, however, prevent CECAMURESA from offering sewing classes for women in 1986.

MEDICAL AND PSYCHOLOGICAL SERVICES

PRIMAS (CASP/Re) applied on behalf of refugees for the health insurance plan (*seguro social*) that was made available to refugees through an agreement between the UNHCR and the Caja Costarricense del Seguro Social signed in July 1982. Several psychologists had their offices within PRIMAS (CASP/Re) and served both refugee adults and children with learning and emotional problems.

A medical doctor located in the OARS office provided services to those refugees who felt they were not given enough attention by Costa Rican doctors or who were not covered by the health insurance plan.[3] A psychologist also consulted there. In addition, OARS offered classes in embroidery as occupational therapy for women. Coordinadora and APTARS (Association of Salvadorean Refugee Professionals and Technicians) administered medical and dental clinics for refugees, and the YMCA hired a psychologist for young men living in the residence discussed below.

RESIDENCE

At the end of 1980 the Episcopalian church placed twenty-nine Salvadorean young men in a Salvation Army hostel. Since living conditions there were poor, the YMCA decided to assume charge of this project and to move the Salvadoreans to another building. In addition, it hired Salvadorean teachers to give classes there. By 1982 the number of Salvadoreans in the project had increased to fifty-six. Young men who had no families living in Costa Rica, who had large families, or whose parents were experiencing problems were eligible to live in the YMCA residence.

In October 1983 the second residence for Salvadorean boys was opened. While the first residence provided food and shelter to young Salvadoreans between seventeen and twenty-three years of age, the second residence was for boys whose age ranged between thirteen and seventeen. A third residence, this time for Salvadorean girls between thirteen and eighteen years of age, was opened in January 1984.

There were no similar residences for adults, except for a refuge created in Fatima Church in June 1980. It offered living quarters to approximately two hundred refugees. This refuge was soon closed and turned into the OARS office.

CULTURAL WORK

Three Salvadorean organizations performed cultural work. The Costa Rican–Salvadorean Cultural Institute (ICCS) was concerned with promoting Salvadorean popular culture and cultural exchange between Costa Ricans and Salvadoreans. It did so by organizing weekly activities. The Cultural Salvadorean Movement (MCS) organized cultural events as well, but its activities were more sporadic. Coordinadora's functions were different: it published a bulletin and participated in a radio program called "Radio de America Latina."

JOB PERMITS

In 1985, when a new unit called the durable solution was created within CASP/Re, one of its functions was to apply for job permits on behalf of refugees to the Mixed Committee, consisting of the Ministry of Labour, the Ministry of Justice, the President's Office, and the Public Security Office. The Mixed Committee reviewed every application and, if an applicant was not replacing a Costa Rican worker, a permit was issued. Only fifty Salvadoreans received job permits under this program in 1986. The first explanation for this low number was Article 13 of the Costa Rican Labour Code, which allowed no more than 10 per cent of workers employed in any particular firm to be foreigners. Second, in order to place refugees in already existing businesses efficiently and without intruding on Costa Rican labour, the Mixed Committee needed to have information on where such demand existed. The Ministry of Labour, however, did not have the necessary funds to conduct an evaluation. In addition to securing job permits, CASP/Re applied to the Mixed Committee for legal permits to establish small urban enterprises.

LEGAL AND RELIGIOUS SERVICES AND DISTRIBUTION OF FOOD

Coordinadora administered a legal aid clinic. A priest who was one of the founders of OARS offered religious services every Sunday and

Table 10
Agencies Promoting Development Projects for Salvadorean Refugees in Costa Rica

Coordinating	*Financing*	*Implementing*
CONAPARE	UNHCR	Caritas
(DIGEPARE)	Project Counselling	Episcopalian church
	Diakonia	OARS
	Catholic Relief Services	YMCA
	EEC	Productor
		PRODES
		APTARS
		ICCS
		Coordinadora
		Econo-Agro
		PRIMAS
		CASP/Re
		INHUDES
		CECAMURESA

on religious holidays. The Episcopalian church organized religious retreat-like workshops (*convivencias*) for refugees.

The Food and Agriculture Organization (FAO) provided food supplements that were distributed by CASP/Re directly to people in rural projects and also through a warehouse in San José. OARS also administered a store selling food at low prices.

DEVELOPMENT PROJECTS

Agencies that offered development aid to refugees in Costa Rica can be divided into three types: government coordinating agencies that define policies with respect to employment programs; international financing agencies that support development projects; and international and domestic agencies that implement them (see table 10).

CONAPARE (National Commission for Refugees) was created in 1980 to define labour policies for refugees to be followed by state institutions and voluntary agencies participating in refugee settlement. However, it carried out no systematic supervision of the durable solution projects in the first two years of the program's implementation. In 1983 CONAPARE conducted an analysis of the economic situation in Costa Rica and proposed to use the 1983 economic development plan, *Volvamos a la Tierra* (Back to the Land), as a guideline for refugee projects. There were several specific criteria for project implementation:

- projects had to be labour intensive;
- they had to be oriented towards transformation of raw materials;
- goods had to be made of national raw materials;
- production had to be directed towards the substitution of imports;
- projects had to satisfy the basic needs of the community in question or society in general;
- they had to be located outside of the metropolitan area of San José but not in distant rural areas close to the northern frontier;
- projects could not replace the national labour force;
- they had to take advantage of the traditional skills of participants; and
- they had to generate enough profit to satisfy the basic needs of participants (CONAPARE 1983a).

In addition, these projects had to be "mixed," that is, they had to include both Costa Rican and Salvadorean workers. Emphasis was placed on agricultural and food-producing enterprises. In the urban field, it was proposed to develop small workshops, specializing mainly in leather goods and clothes. Agricultural projects were to grow basic grains to compensate for the Costa Rican shortage in beans, sorghum, and maize (CONAPARE 1983a).

It was very difficult for implementing agencies to meet these criteria. In 1983 CONAPARE did not approve any projects presented by the voluntary agencies or by PRIMAS. The formation of project proposals was considerably delayed by the requirement to incorporate the national marginal population into the projects for refugees, since there were no resources for the national labour force to match those for refugees. Eventually, this criterion was made optional.

In 1985, as the seriousness of the refugee situation was recognized, CONAPARE, renamed DIGEPARE (General Directorate for Refugees), was moved from the Ministry of Justice to the President's Office. DIGEPARE continued its function of approving employment programs for refugees financed by international voluntary agencies. In addition to the 1983 CONAPARE guidelines, one further criterion dealing with social factors was introduced in 1985. Agencies applying for project approval had to ensure that there was no potential for conflict between the local population and the refugees working in it. This criterion made it difficult for any rural project to be approved. Given the xenophobic feelings characteristic of the Costa Rican population, any rural project, except for those located in an isolated area, had the potential to provoke conflict.

CONAPARE was supposed to direct and assist agencies involved in refugee resettlement. However, apart from setting up some criteria that the agencies found difficult to follow, its role was very weak. DIGEPARE initially showed more interest in a rapprochement with the implementing and financing agencies, but the collaboration did not go beyond three meetings. Agencies that provided funds for development projects included UNHCR, Project Counselling Services for Latin American Refugees, Swedish Ecumenical Action (Diakonia), Catholic Relief Services, and the EEC (European Economic Community) collaborating with DIGEPARE.

When voluntary agencies began to open projects for refugees, they lacked experience in the field. As a result, they made many mistakes, especially in the first two years. Funds were assigned almost at random, market conditions were not investigated, soil and climatic conditions were not tested for rural projects, and recruitment was open so that anyone could apply for a project regardless of job-related skills. In 1983 voluntary agencies began to analyse the reasons for the failure of many of their projects. At the same time, CONAPARE (1983a) conducted its own analysis. It concluded that out of 145 projects, only seventy-one were still active, making the failure rate 51.43 per cent. The report identified several reasons for these poor results:

- poor structure, organization, and planning by implementing agencies;
- migration of beneficiaries to third countries or return to El Salvador;
- interpersonal conflicts;
- irresponsibility of participants;
- health problems; and
- lack of technical and administrative skills among the beneficiaries.

Urban projects had a relatively higher failure rate. Caritas, which specialized in urban projects, reported that eighty-nine of its 129 implemented projects (69 per cent) had failed before June 1983 (Jimenez 1985).

In response to self-scrutiny and evaluations by CONAPARE, implementing agencies hired new members trained as agronomists, economists, or administrators to form technical advisory committees in charge of evaluating project proposals. They also started offering short vocational training and business administration courses to refugees. Technical supervision and control of the projects was strengthened as well.

The new approach did not lead to better results, however. In 1985, when new evaluations were conducted, it was demonstrated that sixty-three out of 152 projects registered with CONAPARE (41.4 per cent) were still active (MIDEPLAN 1985). Thus, 58.6 per cent of the projects had failed. Between 1980 and 1983 Costa Rica was going through an economic crisis that could have affected the economic behaviour of the projects. In 1983, however, the Costa Rican economy began to recover, thus creating more favourable conditions for the implemented projects. In spite of the improved economic context, Salvadorean projects continued going out of business at a high rate. Those enterprises that remained active had lost many of their members. Caritas, for instance, reported that by 1985 membership in still-functioning projects had been reduced by half.

UNHCR signed an agreement with the Catholic Episcopalian Conference through Caritas in October 1981 to finance their durable solution projects. In 1985 an ILO agent evaluated the projects implemented by Caritas, and reported that UNHCR had spent $1,217,759 on them. Administrative spending by Caritas accounted for 34 per cent of this money, making a total direct investment into the projects of $809,658. Given that only 184 beneficiaries were still working in 1985, she calculated that the average investment per refugee was $6618. Consequently, she made a recommendation to terminate the agreement between UNHCR and Caritas (Carrizo 1985). UNHCR accepted this recommendation in December 1985 and signed an agreement with CASP/Re to establish a new local settlement employment program.

In 1981 agencies working with refugees decided that Caritas, financed by UNHCR, would specialize in developing urban projects, while other agencies would be responsible for rural projects. The Project Counselling Service for Latin American Refugees (which received funding from Canadian Inter Pares, Danish Refugee Council, British War on Want, Swedish Heks, the Norwegian Refugee Council, and the Dutch Assistance Fund) made its funds available to the Episcopalian church, OARS, Productor, and PRODES (Popular Projects for Economic and Social Development) for agricultural farms of a cooperative nature. Swedish Diakonia did not maintain any specialization and financed both rural and urban projects. It collaborated with such agencies as Productor, OARS, Econo-Agro, Coordinadora, APTARS, ICCS, and UNHUDES (Institute for Humanism and Development). Participation of the Catholic Relief Services in the resettlement of Salvadorean refugees in Costa Rica was insignificant, and they financed only a few rural projects implemented by OARS in 1983–4.

In 1986 DIGEPARE signed an agreement with the EEC for funding refugee development projects. The EEC had a budget of $2 million to make five hundred families self-sufficient. It established a maximum investment of $4000 per project, which could include several families. DIGEPARE had a team of experts including sociologists, agronomists, psychologists, and economists who, together with two specialists from the EEC, were in charge of project evaluation. Criteria for approval set up by DIGEPARE were so strict that implementing agencies found it difficult to satisfy them, and only two out of twenty-nine projects presented to DIGEPARE for funding were approved in 1986. The other proposals were returned to the implementing agencies for reformulation.[4]

Other international agencies that provided financial support to agencies working with refugees included Irish Trocaire, British OXFAM, British Christian Aid, Dutch Vlusteling, British CAFOD, German Bread for the World, Dutch Stichting, the Swedish World Council of Churches, and others. These agencies did not have offices in Costa Rica but operated from overseas. The projects[5] and agencies administering them are summarized in table 11.

Caritas assumed the function of implementing urban projects in October 1981. By 1985 it had implemented 164 projects, only seventy-four (45.1 per cent) of which had survived (Jimenez 1985). Those projects that were still active had lost half their members. In June 1986 when I interviewed a representative of Caritas, a total of eighty-nine projects existed. Thirty-one had reached self-sufficiency, forty-four were classified by Caritas as "on the road to recovery,"

Table 11
Summary of Projects and Agencies Administering Them

Agency	Implemented projects	Active projects
Caritas	164 urban	89 urban (43 of them Salvadorean)
Episcopalian	10 urban	8 urban
church	12 agricultural	5(?) agricultural
OARS	16 agricultural	4 agricultural
	6 urban	6 urban
Productor	10 agricultural	10 agricultural
YMCA	2 urban	2 urban
PRODES	2 rural coops	2 rural coops
INHUDES	1 agricultural	1 agricultural
Coordinadora/	1 urban	
Econo-Agro	1 agricultural	1 agricultural
APTARS	2 urban	1 urban
ICCS	2 urban	2 urban
CECAMURESA	1 urban	1 urban
PRIMAS	1 rural	1 rural
CASP/Re	100 urban	70(?) urban

and fourteen were classified deficient. Caritas was planning to "liberate" the self-sufficient projects, transfer those on recovery to CASP/Re, and close the others. Of the total number of projects, forty-three were for Salvadorean refugees, providing employment to 114 members. Among them, twenty-nine had reached self-sufficiency, six were on recovery, and eight were deficient. It is not clear what criteria were used for these classifications, since I found that some of the deficient projects were doing economically better (their members reported earning higher salaries) than those in the other categories.

The *Episcopalian church* was the first agency to work with Salvadorean refugees. Assistance began as early as the middle of 1980, before the refugee law had been approved. By 1986 it had implemented twenty-four projects: ten urban, twelve agricultural, and two of religious community work. A total of eighty families joined these projects. Only one urban project benefited Chileans and Guatemalans; the rest were for Salvadorean refugees. The urban projects that were still active in 1986 included a small food store, a coffee stand, two textile workshops, a fabric-weaving project, a shoe vendor, a bakery, and a handicrafts workshop.

Among the twelve agricultural projects by 1986, one had been sold and two clothing stores were purchased with this money. Three projects were still receiving support from the Episcopalian church. One project was sold and it was not clear what its members were doing; another went out of business; and the remaining six had become independent. Two of these projects were functioning well, but members of two others could not subsist on their own farm and were working as agricultural wage-labourers. No information was available on the remaining two farms. Of the ten urban projects, two had gone out of business before 1986 and two went out of business in 1986. The other six were still active.

By January 1985 the *OARS* had implemented twenty-two projects – sixteen agricultural, two small industries, two stores, one housing, and one daycare. When, in December 1985, the OARS was divided in two, thus giving birth to Productor, ten projects remained under the control of OARS. They included four agricultural projects, two small industries, two stores, the daycare centre, and the housing project. One of the stores was located in OARS and sold food to refugees at wholesale prices. The daycare centre offered services to about sixty Salvadorean children. The housing project involved six families (three Salvadorean and three Costa Rican) who received funds to build themselves houses. Twenty-four people were employed in the remaining seven projects.

In 1983 the *YMCA* opened three projects – a carpentry, tailoring, and electrical repair shop. The YMCA purchased machinery for the electrical repair shop, but the Ministry of Labour did not grant it a licence. The project had to be closed before it even started. The carpentry workshop was to include twelve people – ten Salvadoreans and two Costa Ricans. The Costa Rican members decided not to join at the last minute. Out of the ten original members of the workshop, seven were still working there in 1986. They also had one new member join the project. The tailoring workshop was designed for eleven members only, four of whom had stayed for about a year and then left. Four new members were put into the project in 1985 and they were still working there in 1986. The project was experiencing some serious financial problems at the time and hoped to receive refinancing from Productor, given that the Norwegian Project Council (which originally financed the project) refused more aid.

PRODES was formed in March 1986. It emerged as a response to an evaluation of rural projects by a team of experts who concluded that rather than creating new job projects for refugees, it made more sense to incorporate them into already existing cooperatives. Agency representatives approached several Costa Rican cooperatives and two of them agreed to accept some refugees. One agricultural cooperative, located in the province of Limon, had room for ten Salvadorean refugees, but PRODES had serious difficulty finding Salvadoreans who were willing to join it. The prolonged UNHCR assistance produced some negative repercussions. Those refugees who came from rural areas of El Salvador got accustomed to what the city could offer them, facilities such as electricity, running tap water, and medical services. They no longer wanted to join rural projects. After a long search, ten families were found. PRODES hoped to incorporate ten other families (five Salvadorean and five Costa Rican) in the cooperative in 1987 and to do the same in 1988.

While this project allowed ten Salvadorean families to start earning a living, Costa Rican members of this cooperative benefited as well. PRODES persuaded the Ministry of Health to install a medical post in the area and to open a daycare centre to control children's diet and allow women to join in production. The Ministry of Education agreed to expand the already existing school. CASP/Re and the UNHCR donated some wood-heated stoves to the cooperative. A Salvadorean cabinet maker was hired to teach the cooperative members to make basic furniture for themselves. The Canadian Cooperation (a program promoting cooperatives) donated a tractor at PRODES's request.

The second project was similar. Ten young Salvadorean men were incorporated into a cooperative of young fishermen. As in the case of the first project, ten more members were expected to join the cooperative in both 1987 and 1988. The two projects received financial help in the form of a loan and a donation.

The Institute for Humanism and Development implemented only one rural project in Costa Rica (its major areas of operation were primarily El Salvador and then Nicaragua), but it did other work that was related to development projects. INHUDES tried to raise the consciousness of refugees already incorporated into projects implemented by OARS, since most Salvadoreans were thought to be individualistic and therefore had problems working in group projects. INHUDES felt it was important to organize seminars in order to develop a cooperative spirit among these refugees. In 1985 it organized five workshops, attended by two to three hundred people, in the hope that these seminars would enable the Salvadoreans attending them to work smoothly in projects.

The *Coordinadora for Salvadorean Refugees* was formed in 1981. In cooperation with Econo-Agro, it started two productive projects in 1985. Only one of them was still active in 1986.

APTARS implemented one tailoring workshop for three Salvadorean refugees that went out of business three months later. It also ran one small restaurant.

The *Costa Rican–Salvadorean Cultural Institute* was primarily concerned with promoting Salvadorean culture and cultural exchange between Costa Ricans and Salvadoreans. In order to continue offering cultural activities, it decided to open two productive projects which, it was hoped, would generate funds for these activities. The two projects were a small restaurant serving Salvadorean food and a Salvadorean crafts workshop. In 1986 the projects were still unable to generate profit to be used for cultural functions.

Finally, CECAMURESA formed a small productive workshop including three seamstresses. By the time I had completed my research, the workshop had not reached self-sufficiency.

PRIMAS administered only one rural project, Los Angeles, which was the largest rural project in Costa Rica and the first one of its kind in Latin America. Many people viewed it as a model for refugee resettlement. However, hopes for the project soon turned sour. The history of this project dates back to May 1980 when two hundred Salvadorean peasants occupied the Costa Rican embassy in San Salvador and, as a result, were granted asylum by the Costa Rican government. They were settled in stables on a farm, called Murcielago, a former property of Anastacio Somoza, a Nicaraguan deposed dictator. Living conditions on the farm were deplorable. Moreover, the proximity of Nicaraguan contras put the lives of these Salvadoreans in danger. As a result of complaints, refugees were moved to a 191-hectare farm, called Los Angeles, located in the north of Costa Rica, purchased by UNHCR in December 1980. The farm had potential to offer a viable future to many more refugees, and by May 1981 some four hundred people had been settled on it. Many of them were coerced to join when they were threatened with having their assistance cut off if they refused. Consequently, some Salvadoreans were afraid even to apply for refugee status owing to the rumour that every refugee would be sent to Los Angeles by force. Plans were made to buy an additional one thousand hectares on which to settle a total of 7000 Salvadoreans (*Denuncia y Solidaridad* 1981, 4). Fortunately for Salvadoreans, this plan never materialized. The maximum ever settled on the farm was around one thousand people, most of whom left because of bad living conditions. Various sources reported shortages of food, medical care, neglect of psychological needs, and poor hygiene on the farm (*Denuncia y Solidaridad* 1981; *Universidad Semanal*, no. 492, 1981). Since the living conditions in Los Angeles were precarious, forty refugees decided to leave. The Costa Rican Ministry of Justice responded by sending a letter to all agencies in charge of refugees, telling them not to offer any kind of emergency aid to the fugitives. In spite of this threat, many other refugees followed their example and left the farm. In 1985 twenty families, mostly women with children, were still living in Los Angeles.

CASP/Re replaced PRIMAS in 1985 and was in charge of administering small urban projects. Since it did not keep in touch with the project beneficiaries after giving them money, it was difficult to find out how many of these projects were still active. I estimate that out of one hundred Salvadorean beneficiaries of this assistance, about seventy were still operative at the time of my research. Out of the forty-nine individual Salvadorean recipients of this program whom I could interview, only eleven (22 per cent) were working full-time in the occupation for which they had received the donation. Seventeen (35 per cent) dedicated part of their time to working in the financed businesses, and twenty-one (43 per cent) were not using machinery or tools they had received through the program at all.

According to an evaluation conducted by Amanda Carrizo, the proponent of the program, its failure rate was only 25.4 per cent (Carrizo 1986). The discrepancy with the results of my study is significant. When I presented my results to Carrizo, she suggested that the difference could be explained by the fact that her evaluation included both Nicaraguans Salvadoreans while my research dealt with Salvadoreans only. According to Carrizo, Nicaraguans were more successful businessmen than Salvadoreans. While this may be true to some extent, I believe that other factors also produced the difference in results in our studies. The evaluation directed by Carrizo was conducted by social workers from CASP/Re, the government agency administering the program. Those refugees who were not employing their machinery or tools for business were afraid to admit it for fear of confiscation by the government agency. Those refugees who had sold the machinery, raw materials, or tools were afraid of sanctions. This explains why the failure rate could have been underreported in Carrizo's research.

In sum, there were approximately 350 people working in the employment projects administered by various agencies in 1986. In addition, fifty people had received job permits to work as wage-labourers. In other words, some 400 Salvadoreans were incorporated into the local economy. At the same time, those between twenty and sixty years of age made up 78 per cent of the Salvadorean refugee population, or approximately 4500 people. Thus, less than 10 per cent of Salvadorean adults were given employment by the agencies. Some 90 per cent of Salvadorean refugees had to rely on self-help in order to survive.

THE PROCESS OF PROJECT APPROVAL

What was the process of project approval? It took three months for the agency's team of experts to evaluate proposals. Caritas could decide on their fate on its own, while other agencies had to send proposals to the financing agencies. The latter, in their turn, evaluated proposed projects and, if approved, sent application forms to the international financing agencies overseas. While the criteria for approval by implementing and financing agencies in Costa Rica had to do with the economic profitability of a proposed project, overseas financing agencies based their decision mainly on the availability of funds. Except for the projects implemented by Caritas, it generally took six to nine months for a proposal to be approved. In the case of Caritas, the process lasted three months. This lengthy procedure created problems, because some of the potential beneficiaries did not wish to wait so long and found other employment in the meantime. Thus, new members had to be found, and this delayed project implementation even further.

The advantage of the local settlement program implemented by CASP/Re was its relatively speedy process of approval of applications for small businesses. It lasted only about a month. It was rapid because there were few decisions to be made. The amount of a grant corresponded to occupational categories outlined in a table used by the agency's social workers. Since all businesses were urban, there was no need for a study of soil and climatic conditions. The decision on what occupational groups could be approved was made in advance. The only criterion used for approval (apart from being a "convention" refugee) was previous job experience. And even that was not often required.

It is not clear whether implementing agencies had more weight than the financing agencies in reaching a decision on a project proposal. Usually, a good degree of interaction existed between the two so that if a financing agency found faults in a proposal, it was returned to the implementing agency for correction. After projects were approved, it became the responsibility of implementing agencies to administer them. Only if further refinancing was required was the assistance of the financing agencies solicited.

Financial assistance to the projects had been offered in the form of grants until 1986, when all the agencies agreed that refugees would identify more with the projects and would feel more responsible for them if they were given loans instead. Starting that year (and in some cases even earlier), refugees incorporated into projects received loans.

In sum, Salvadorean refugees in Costa Rica benefited from a large number of assistance projects that tried to cover economic needs (relief aid, food distribution, development projects, and job permits), as well as medical, psychological, cultural, legal, and housing needs. Chapters 5 to 8 analyse only the employment creation programs.

5 Durable Solution
and Local Settlement
Urban Employment Programs

Because refugees abandon their means of subsistence in their own countries, they become more dependent on various governmental and voluntary agencies that provide them with resources required for survival. Institutional assistance is of crucial importance to those refugees who are not allowed to participate freely in the economy of the host country. Since most refugee asylum countries control access to their labour markets, it becomes important to understand how to make institutional aid effective. Insufficient aid or inadequate delivery can result in high failure rates among development schemes.

The local settlement program was a response to the high failure rate of the durable solution projects. This new program was based on a different notion of urban development. Instead of promoting large refugee projects, it aimed at establishing businesses that would be much smaller in terms of initial investment and membership. Was local settlement a more successful program?

I compared thirty-seven durable solution (DS) and thirty local settlement (LS) projects in this study. Major differences between these two programs are summarized in table 12. The initial investment per capita in DS projects is significantly higher than the investment per LS recipient (63,314 colones and 13,855 colones, respectively). When total investment per capita is calculated as a sum of initial investment and refinancing, the disparity between the two programs becomes even more pronounced (71,197 colones and 13,855 colones,

Table 12
Major Differences between Durable Solution and Local Settlement Programs

	Local settlement	Durable solution
Average monthly income	5,380	8,080
Average adjusted monthly income	6,570	7,540
Investment per capita	13,855	63,314
Total investment per capita	13,855	71,197
Average number of workers per business	1.27	3.73
Average number of jobs per business	0.80	3.32
Total number of workers	38	138
Number of owners	30	74
Number of wage-labourers	1	29
Number of paid family labourers	6	19
Number of unpaid family labourers	0	5
Number of apprentices	0	11

respectively). The average investment per capita in the LS program is less than one-fifth of that in DS projects. At the same time, an average adjusted income per DS project member is 7540 colones per month while those in the LS program is 6570 colones per month, the latter being 87 per cent of the former. In terms of cost efficiency the LS program demonstrated much better results and, in absolute terms, those in the LS program earned only slightly less. Moreover, if instead of receiving a grant from an agency refugees had to borrow money from a bank, their adjusted incomes would be 6400 colones per month in the case of LS recipients and only 5810 colones per month in the case of DS beneficiaries (calculation of the debt is explained in the appendix). Overall, then, the LS program demonstrated better results.

Adjusted incomes, however, were calculated on the basis of what the income would be if small enterprises worked forty-five hours per week, provided there was regular demand. There were considerably more beneficiaries of the LS than the DS program who worked less than forty-five hours per week in their businesses (see table 13). Real average incomes were over 8080 colones and 5380 colones for the DS and LS programs, respectively. In other words, while some LS projects had the potential for offering income compatible with that earned by DS beneficiaries, their owners preferred to avoid the risk of investing their entire time in these businesses and continued to work in other jobs as well.

Table 13
Hours Worked Per Week by Project Beneficiaries

Hours	Durable solution	Local settlement
	(per cent)	
Less than 20	3	30
20–30	0	17
30–45	40	30
More than 45	57	23

With respect to generation of employment, seventy-four DS project members created employment for twenty-nine wage-labourers, eleven apprentices, and nineteen paid family members. In contrast, LS project members created employment for only one wage-labourer, one apprentice, and six family members. One DS project member with an average investment of 71,197 colones hired 0.80 workers. One LS member with an average investment of 13,855 colones employed 0.27 workers (unpaid family workers were not taken into account). Employment of one worker costs 20,366 colones in DS projects, and 10,938 colones in the LS projects.[1] When employment was calculated with respect to the number of hours worked per week (eg, a worker engaged in the business for thirty hours was equated with a 0.7 job), the difference between the cost of jobs for the two programs became considerably smaller. The LS program created 23.9 jobs or an average of 0.80 jobs per enterprise at a cost of 17,318 colones per job, while the DS program created 122.7 jobs or an average of 3.32 jobs per project at a cost of 21,445 colones per job. While in relative terms employment in the DS program was somewhat more costly, in absolute terms the LS program can hardly be considered successful since it did not create sufficient employment (less than one fully employed person per enterprise).

Does higher investment per project translate into higher salary earned by a program participant? Statistically, the correlation between total investment per capita and present income is insignificant ($N = 62$, $P = -0.05$, $p > 0.07$). As will be demonstrated later, high investments in some projects did not enable their members to earn good salaries. Smaller investments, however, often provided sufficient income opportunities for program participants. A financial investment is only one factor that influences the economic performance of small businesses. It is important for projects that require machinery.

Table 14
Occupational Composition of Salvadorean Enterprises, by Employment Program

Occupation	Durable solution	Local settlement
Shoemaking/repair	3	5
Clothesmaking/repair	11	8
Bakery	4	6
Soda	5	1
Services	1	3
Carpentry	3	2
Leather	1	0
Mechanics	3	3
Crafts	3	1
Commerce	2	0
Other	1	1
Total	37	30

Another significant factor is location, which is especially important for those enterprises that produce directly for a client. Even when investments in machinery are adequate and location is good, an enterprise may still do poorly because of lack of demand or skill.

There was a significant range of income within the durable solution and the local settlement projects. In order to understand the interaction between three variables – machinery, skills, and demand (which in some cases depends on location) – it is useful to divide all the enterprises according to the occupational category to which they belong (see table 14) and to compare the two programs within each category.

Shoemakers sell their products to stores and the type of neighbourhood they live in is not important to marketing their product. They require a special leather sewing machine to be able to make shoes. With the exception of one, all shoe-making DS projects were equipped with the necessary machinery. Only one DS recipient claimed that his project was "desgraciado" (unfortunate) since it had received no machinery. Those who benefited from the LS system received only raw materials. All the LS shoemakers under study, however, had already established their businesses or had been working in shoe workshops as wage-labourers prior to receiving assistance. Two of them continued working part-time in Costa Rican workshops and could use the workshop machinery to make shoes for their own businesses. Other people were able to acquire a sewing machine from their own savings or as a present from foreign friends. Disregarding the case of one family where production was significantly impaired by the mental illness of the family head, the average income of shoemakers was 10,216 colones per month. There was no significant income difference between those in LS and those in DS projects. In fact, when hours of work were taken into consideration, LS recipients were found to be doing better than those in the DS program. Adjusted average income was 10,490 colones per month for those in the LS programs and 6900 colones for DS recipients. The latter was low because of the effect of the DS project with no machinery whose two owners were each making only 4300 colones per month. Those in the LS program were able to generate a similar or better income because they themselves had found solutions to the problem of obtaining machinery, and not because of the aid received through the LS.

One LS recipient who did not have access to a machine devoted himself to shoe repair. The demand was very low in his neighbourhood for this type of work. He did not want to move to a more central location, however, because he would have to pay a higher rent. He was making 2400 colones per month repairing shoes and had to work full-time elsewhere to survive.

In textile production, as well as in bakeries, there was a significant income difference between those who had been put in a DS project and those who were LS beneficiaries. In DS projects, small textile producers made 8350 colones per month on an average while seamstresses in the LS program earned 2540 colones per month (adjusted average monthly income being 7950 and 3670 colones, respectively). An average monthly income of bakers in DS projects was 10,000 colones, as compared to 3500 colones for those in the LS (14,730 and 4220 colones, respectively, when adjusted with respect to hours and demand). This contrast can be explained by the different amounts of investment into the two programs.

When the durable solution projects were implemented, an average investment in capital equipment was 38,650 colones. An average investment in machinery per LS project (where applicable) was 11,300 colones.[2] In the meantime, the DS projects under study were significantly reduced in size. Those who remained in the projects kept some valuable machinery of an industrial and semi-industrial nature. They did not keep all the machinery donated to the project, as some surplus was confiscated by the agencies in charge. The machinery offered to people in the LS, in contrast, was of a domestic nature. Seamstresses got household sewing machines that were very slow and did not allow them to finish the edging well. Finishing is usually done by a special machine called an "overlock," which was generally provided to the durable solution projects. The stoves given to bakers in the LS program were not suitable for profitable baking as they consumed a lot of energy and, because of their small size, made production slow. These factors hampered the LS producers' ability to compete with other small seamstresses and bakers.

When DS projects were implemented, the first few months of rent were paid for them. That gave their members an opportunity to find a location in a relatively good neighbourhood. When the assistance was cut off, they had already had a chance to establish a clientele and could then continue paying the rent on their own.

The situation was different with LS recipients. When the LS program began at the end of 1985, it was designed to create employment mainly for the heads of family. This included many single mothers who had not yet been integrated into any project. These people had survived on UNHCR assistance and occasional illegal jobs. Their income had been low, so they had to live in inexpensive houses in poor neighbourhoods. The LS programs offered them a machine or tools and/or raw materials but no chance to move out of their neighbourhood. Although these small producers saw their location as an impediment to their businesses' survival, they nevertheless did not want to take the risk of moving out of inexpensive houses. Their immediate clients, therefore, were low-income people who did not generate sufficient demand for custom-made goods, who paid little, and even that on credit.

Those who received LS assistance often had to join the program as they were losing their emergency aid. The CASP/Re social workers tried to integrate them into the labour force, at times ignoring their actual skills. It was assumed that any woman could sew and bake, and many of them were given a sewing machine or a stove. It turned out, however, that their domestic skills were not sufficient to make their businesses work well.

Among members of the twenty-two failed LS projects, thirteen were seamstresses and three were bakers. Eight seamstresses had no previous labour experience in textiles and only some rudimentary sewing skills. Out of those seamstresses and bakers with an LS donation who were still working in 1986, two bakers and two seamstresses had no previous experience in the field and were earning as little as 2925 colones per month on average.

There were two LS recipients who, because they could not produce clothes competitively, devoted themselves to clothes repair. Demand for these services was low, especially in poor neighbourhoods, and so were incomes generated in this occupation (less than 2500 colones per month).

In other occupations there were no sharp differences between refugees in DS projects and those who had received LS assistance. Painters, repairers, electricians, and subcontractors working in construction (masons and carpenters) did not require capital investment. Some basic tools and possibly some raw materials were sufficient inputs. Neither did they depend on the location of the business since, apart from construction subcontractors and watch repairers, they provided services at the home of a client (a domicilio). They did, however, require skills. If they already possessed the skills, a donation offered by the LS program was sufficient. In the sample, all those who received LS assistance in the above-mentioned occupations were earning a healthy income (between 9000 and 16,000 colones per month). Two painters were an exception. Both of them had just started their businesses and did not yet have a good clientele. Even by working just a few hours, however, they were able to earn good incomes. One painter, for instance, earned 6000 colones in eight hours.

In some occupational categories, even well-financed projects produced low incomes. While the construction carpenter was earning 12,000 colones monthly, all carpentry workshops were experiencing problems as competition with industrially produced furniture was considerable. One carpentry workshop, for instance, received 1.2 million colones from the implementing agency. Its six members were earning a maximum of 5500 colones per month when they had work, and at times they did not earn anything at all. Another carpentry project, with a total investment of 750,000 colones for six people, provided its members with a salary of 2000 colones per month. If the money given to these two projects had been borrowed from a bank, their members' salary would have been negative. A TV and radio repair workshop consisting of two members received 130,000 colones from the implementing agency, but was able to earn only 2200 colones per month for each member by subcontracting work from a Costa Rican workshop. And the auto mechanical shop, which had received 150,000 colones for four people, had only one original member left, who was earning 5000 per month.

LOCAL SETTLEMENT, DURABLE SOLUTION, AND GENDER DIFFERENCES

Among the Salvadoreans I interviewed, there were almost four times more male than female owners who benefited from the DS program. In the LS program, however, there were roughly as many men as there were women (see table 15). These findings are hardly surprising. The gender-based division between domestic life and public domain (work) is prevalent in Latin America. In the absence of a state daycare system, women are often forced to take jobs that allow them to work for money and take care of their children at the same time. The DS program financed projects outside the home and made it difficult for many women to join them. By contrast, the LS program provided small assistance to refugees that enabled them to work at home. Since absolute results of the LS program were poor in comparison with those of the DS, Salvadorean women in urban projects had lower incomes. While men earned on an average 7284 colones per month, women earned 5438 colones or 25 per cent less than the men. When adjusted income is calculated, the difference is 30 per cent, with men earning on an average 8028 and women 5576 colones per month.

SMALL ENTERPRISES WITHOUT INSTITUTIONAL ASSISTANCE

An analysis of the influence of institutional assistance on the economic performance of small enterprises would not be complete without a comparison with those enterprises established without institutional assistance (*por cuenta propia*). I only found eight such enterprises. Although the number is small, some conclusions can nevertheless be drawn from the analysis.

Three of the enterprises had low input requirements. They included one crafts workshop, a street jewel vendor, and a soapmaker. The

Table 15
Participation in Local Settlement and Durable Solution Programs by Gender

Gender	Local settlement	Durable solution
	(frequency)	
Men	14	57
Women	16	17

Source: Survey of 104 owners of sixty-seven Salvadorean refugee projects

first workshop, consisting of three people, received a private loan of 10,000 colones from a friend (with easy repayment terms). The second business started with an investment of 5000 colones received as a donation from the YMCA. Despite this donation, the enterprise was not considered as a "project" because the YMCA did not try to control its further development. I did not obtain information on the initial investment by the soapmaker, but it could not have been high since he had only a few tubs and barrels and no machinery. Members of these three enterprises had a relatively good monthly salary, being 7500 colones in the case of three craftsmen and the jewel vendor, and 20,000 colones for the soapmaker. The latter worked sixty-six hours per week and, if he had had a machine to cut soap, his productivity would have been higher and he would not have had to work so much.

A photographer's story is different. He required substantial investment to purchase a camera and materials. A political party to which he belonged agreed to purchase these for him so he could take pictures of their political functions. At the same time, the photographer could serve a regular clientele and earn a relatively good income (about 7500 colones per month).

Two tailors did not have sufficient funds to establish stable businesses. One of them managed to buy two second-hand sewing machines for 10,000 colones. The other was using his friend's sewing machine, which must have cost no more than 5000 colones. Both tailors did maquila (subcontracting from larger enterprises). While the first one subcontracted only during the two months of high demand (November and December), the second one did it throughout the year. The first earned 14,000 colones monthly (working seventy hours per week) during the busy months and only 2000 colones per month when no maquila was available. The second earned about

5600 colones per month all year. If these tailors had better machinery, they would have been able to sell to stores or private customers, thus increasing their sales. Even if they continued subcontracting, better sewing machines would have increased their productivity and resulted in better earnings.

The case of one bakery owner was quite exceptional. His wife started the business by making pastries at home and selling them in the street, while he worked in a bakery project. When he left the project (because of interpersonal conflicts) and joined his wife's enterprise, the demand for their product was high and, as a result, their business grew rapidly. In three years they invested about 250,000 colones in their enterprise.

A conclusion drawn from this analysis of enterprises without institutional assistance is similar to what was found in the case of projects administered by various institutions. There were those enterprises that could function well with a low initial investment, as well as those that generated low incomes if they were undercapitalized.

CONCLUSIONS

The issue of institutional assistance is crucial in the development of both refugee projects and the informal sector in general. The examination of the two employment programs indicates that availability of more assistance does not necessarily translate into a higher success rate. The amount of help given should be tailored to the requirements of each business. Some occupations function very well with the type of assistance offered through local settlement. They include painters, electricians, construction masons and carpenters, and to a lesser degree watch repairers. These occupations require an input of tools and some raw materials, but no machinery. They are not dependent on the location of the business.

Those occupations that require input in machinery (shoemakers, seamstresses, tailors, and bakers) cannot survive when they are offered cheap machinery of the domestic type. Those producers who cater to private customers in their immediate neighbourhood – seamstresses, tailors, and bakers – depend on location for their business to succeed. They need assistance to locate themselves well. Those shoemakers who are given no machinery at all, and are therefore expected to repair shoes, need to be centrally located. However, that means having to pay high rent, and without institutional assistance a small producer who is starting her or his business is not able to afford it. Carpentry workshops, even when well financed, face strong competition with the industrial sector, and do not provide their members with adequate incomes. Individual carpenters, subcontracting in construction, do considerably better.

PART THREE

Explaining Survival and Relative Success of Salvadorean Urban Enterprises

6 Petty Commodity Production: Dissolution and Conservation

INFORMAL SECTOR VERSUS PETTY COMMODITY PRODUCTION

Small urban enterprises, similar to those created for Salvadorean refugees in Costa Rica, have been analysed as informal by some and as petty commodity production by others. Those who view them as informal are interested in distinguishing them from formal enterprises. Those who regard them as petty commodity production emphasize those characteristics that contrast them to capitalist enterprises. Even though the two concepts refer to different phenomena, there is an overlap in the characteristics to which they refer. Some writers, as will be seen later, use the two concepts interchangeably.

The concept of the informal sector, as opposed to the formal sector, was introduced by Hart (1970). It was used to draw a distinction between wage earning and self-employment. Hart characterized the informal sector as an unorganized, unenumerated, and low-income sector. The concept of the informal sector was adopted by the International Labour Office (ILO) and applied to their policy-oriented study of employment opportunities in Kenya (ILO, 1972). Their report identified the following characteristics of the informal sector: ease of entry into the activity concerned; reliance on indigenous resources; family ownership of enterprises; small scale of operation;

labour-intensive technology; skills acquired outside the formal school system; and unregulated yet competitive market. Alternatively, the formal sector was characterized by blocked entry; reliance on imported resources; corporate ownership; large-scale operations in markets protected by tariffs, quotas, and trade licences; and use of capital-intensive and often imported technology and of workers with formally acquired skills. The ILO mission described people in the informal sector as having low income and choosing informal activities as a result of their failure to integrate into formal activities. Although the concept has been widely used, many authors have criticized it for a number of reasons.

First, there is a structural overlap between the two sectors, making it difficult to draw a clear-cut line between them (Harriss 1978; Bromley 1985). Second, some of the traits associated with the informal sector are not universal (House 1984; Peattie 1980; Wellings and Sutcliffe 1984). Third, the informal sector is so heterogeneous that it is impossible to group all enterprises within it under the same category (Moser 1977; LeBrun and Gerry 1975). And, finally, as argued by several authors (Moser 1978; Castells and Portes 1989; Beneria 1989), the dual model that draws a distinction between the two sectors undermines the existence of complex relations between them.

Therefore, more recent studies (Portes, Castells, and Benton 1989) have moved away from defining the two sectors. Instead, they define informality as a characteristic that can apply to small-scale enterprises as well as to modern industries. First, informality refers to the unregulated nature of organization – namely, noncompliance with official and administrative requirements of registration and tax (Roberts 1989, 41; Beneria 1989, 184; Ybarra 1989, 217)[1] and with government labour regulations and welfare provisions (Castells and Portes 1989, 13; Roberts 1989, 43). Additionally, informal activities are believed to be carried out without work contracts or with purely temporary ones. Remuneration is "in kind" or by piece rate, rather than by a fixed wage (Robers 1989, 43; Ybarra 1989, 217). From this perspective, informality characterizes not only small underme-chanized enterprises that occupy the bottom of the ladder in the urban economy, but also the most modern of firms (Roberts 1989, 43; Castells and Portes 1989, 12).

Some students of the so-called informal economy preferred moving away from this concept and instead view small urban enterprises as petty commodity production (Moser 1978; Gerry 1979; LeBrun and Gerry 1975). Petty commodity production is defined as a transitional form between noncapitalist and capitalist models of production. The main characteristics of petty commodity production are that it is small-scale, linked to commodity exchange, and relatively independent in terms of ownership and control of the means of production, with little separation between capital and labour. There has been general agreement among scholars (Friedmann 1980; Smith 1984; Goodman and Redclift 1985; Chevalier 1982; Bernstein 1988) that petty commodity producers can be distinguished from such noncapitalist forms of economy as peasantry by virtue of their commoditization. Yet there is a disagreement on whether this commoditization involves only their relation with the market or, in addition, their internal relations of production. Thus for Friedmann (1980), although wage labour may exist in petty commodity production units, it is only of a temporary nature. By and large, petty commodity producers do not hire labour. Chevalier (1982), in contrast, believes that internal relations among simple commodity producers are equally commodified. Smith (1984, 82) maintains that rather than the absence of wage labour as such, the defining feature of simple commodity production "should be the absence of a fully proletarianized, self-reproducing labour force."

Others, like Goodman and Redclift (1985, 238), for instance, avoid generalizing about simple commodity production. They contend that it is a "historically contingent phenomenon, which consequently can be expected to undergo significant transformation and variation in the course of capitalist development." Similarly, Lem maintains that social relations among petty commodity producers may be characterized by a mixture of commodified and noncommodified features, and that this stems from the unevenness of capitalist penetration in all spheres of production. She argues that there is "partial" commodification of social relations both within and between households and that mobilization of household members remains an essential structural feature of petty commodity production (Lem 1988, 503).

The petty commodity form[2] of production includes traditional and modern artisanal production, peasant agriculture, and various services such as small-scale trade and transport (Long and Richardson 1978). Moser (1978) believes that most of the small enterprises usually characterized as informal would fit into the category of petty commodity production. I would also argue that most petty commodity producers avoid contractual labour and marketing relations and can be characterized as informal. Moser argues that the contribution of the petty commodity approach was to shift the emphasis from defining the two sectors to understanding the interrelation between them (Moser 1978, 1055). Yet the concept of informality does not preclude one from analysing the relationship between small urban enterprises and capitalist firms (see Portes, Castells, and Benton 1989, for instance). What is the nature of the relationship between informal noncapitalist and capitalist enterprises?

Answers to this question can be classified into three approaches. According to the first, noncapitalist forms of production are gradually replaced by capitalist forms (Marx 1970). This view is challenged by the persistence of noncapitalist forms of production in the capitalist economy. The second approach regards the capitalist penetration in underdeveloped countries as being temporarily retarded by the existing pre-capitalist forms of production (Bettelheim 1972; Wolpe 1972; Wallerstein 1977). According to the third approach, noncapitalist and capitalist relationships coexist without ever disappearing (Gershuny 1979; LeBrun and Gerry 1975; Bradby 1975).

PRE-CAPITALIST FORMS OF PRODUCTION: DISSOLUTION AND CONSERVATION

One interpretation, based on Marx's earlier works on European countries, views capitalism as encroaching on pre-capitalist societies and triggering a process of primitive accumulation. This process, according to orthodox Marxists, is unilineal and eventually results in the complete separation of direct producers from ownership of the means of production. This dissolution of pre-capitalist relationships is viewed as inevitable. Marx writes for instance that:

Wherever it takes root capitalist production destroys all forms of commodity production which are based either on the self-employment of producers, or merely on the sale of excess product as commodities ... capitalist production first makes the production of commodities general and then, by degrees, transforms all commodity production into capitalist production (Marx 1970, 36).

Later in his life, Marx redefined his views on the destruction of the pre-capitalist forms of production with the advent of capitalism. Thus, in volume 2 of *Capital* he states:

No matter whether commodities are the output of production based on slavery, of peasants ... or of half-savage hunting tribes, etc. ... as commodities and money they come face to face with the money and commodities in which the industrial capital presents itself ... The character of the process of production from which it originates is immaterial. They function as commodities in the market, and as commodities they enter into the circuit of industrial capital as well as into the circulation of surplus value incorporated into it ... To replace them ... they must be reproduced and to this extent the capitalist mode of production is conditional on modes of production lying outside of its own stage of development (Marx 1962, 109–10).

Abundant evidence demonstrates that the pre-capitalist forms of production are very much alive in the developing countries. Bettelheim (1972, 297) argues that where the capitalist mode is not pervasive, noncapitalist forms of production are simultaneously restructured (partly dissolved) and subordinated to the predominant capitalist relations (and so conserved).

Most authors who discuss the dissolution-conservation thesis (Miras 1980; Leonard 1980; Dewar and Watson 1982; McGee 1979; and Tokman 1978) do not state clearly which of the two processes, dissolution or conservation, predominates. Some of them do, however, express the belief that the pre-capitalist forms of production gradually disappear.

Bettelheim (1972), for instance, views the process of conservation as retarding but not permanently preserving the pre-capitalist economies. This view is shared by Wolpe. He observes that during the earlier stages of capitalist development in South Africa, the rate of capital accumulation depended on the maintenance of pre-capitalist relations of production in the economy of the migrant labour force on the reserves. Wolpe (1972, 432) goes on to say:

This relationship between the two modes of production, however, is contradictory and increasingly produces the conditions which make impossible the continuation of the pre-capitalist relations of production in the Reserves. The consequence of this is the accelerating dissolution of these relations and the development, within Africa, towards a single, capitalist, mode of production.

In the late 1970s, Wallerstein (1977, 38) predicted that "in about 1990, or whenever the world economy expands again, the proletarisation of the work force, may become virtually universal."

Yet other authors believe that pre-capitalist forms of production persist. Gershuny (1979), for instance, argues that it is "wholly misleading" to picture economic development as a one-way progress, as a transition from a traditional to a modern society. On the basis of his analysis of an industrial society (England), he contends, "we have to consider a whole series of little transformations of production, perhaps taking place simultaneously, between the formal economy, the household or communal sector, and the underground sector, whose directions are determined by the particular social and technical conditions pertaining to the production of particular commodities at particular points in time" (Gershuny 1979, 9).

Wellings and Sutcliffe believe that conservation and dissolution mechanisms interplay and maintain pre-capitalist forms of production at an "optimal" size. With respect to the informal sector, Wellings and Sutcliffe (1984, 540–1) write:

Thus as far as formal sector capitalists are concerned, the informal sector should not become so small that the rising cost of the reproduction of labour begins to have a significant effect upon wages, or so small that they begin to suffer from lost enterprise in the low-income market, or so small that its effect upon the unemployment problem is minimal. At the same time, though, it must not develop to such a size that it becomes competitive in the formal market.

Bradby (1975, 129–30) draws attention to the importance of historical conditions:

As this theory assumes neither universal destructiveness on the part of capitalism nor a general tendency towards the preservation of precapitalist modes of production, the task of analysis will be to discover what are the historical conditions which lead to either of these tendencies in particular cases.

LeBrun and Gerry (1975, 29) observe that while the dissolution aspect dominates over conservation in developed countries, in developing or peripheral countries it is the conservation aspect that dominates. This argument is contradicted by the evidence of recent trends towards informalization of the economy in industrial countries (Portes, Castells, and Benton 1989).

Why do pre-capitalist forms of production survive (whether temporarily or permanently) and even re-emerge? Neo-Marxist scholars have advanced two types of explanations: the dependency and the articulation approaches.

The Dependency School

Dependency is defined as a situation in which capitalist development in some countries or some sectors of a country's economy constrains the growth of underdeveloped sectors (Goodman and Redclift 1981, 47). Frank (1970) criticizes the model that views the two parts of the world economic system (developed and underdeveloped countries) as each having a history, a structure, and a contemporary dynamic largely independent of the other. He argues that the economic growth in the metropolis or core (developed countries) is contingent upon the underdevelopment of the satellite or periphery (underdeveloped countries).

The dependency model, popularized by Frank (1970) and elaborated by Cardoso (1972), Dos Santos (1970), Furtado (1971), and others, has been widely criticized for its failure to account for heterogeneity among the "underdeveloped" countries, for its neglect of internal conditions, and its dualistic perspective (Blomstrom and Hettne 1984; Booth 1975; O'Brien 1975). Moreover, the dependency model cannot account for the re-emergence of pre-capitalist forms of production in capitalist economies.

Laclau (1971) criticizes Frank for dispensing with the "relations of production" in his definition of capitalism. For Laclau, the mechanism of creation of dependency has to be understood at the level of production. He argues that to sustain the process of accumulation, capitalism requires expansion of productive units in which either low technology or low wages counteract the tendency for profit rates to decline. Investment in production in the peripheral areas offers an opportunity for developed capitalism to move in. In feudal or slave productive units, such as plantations or haciendas, organic composition of capital is low and the labour force, which is abundant and cheap, is subject to forms of extra-economic coercion. In this sense, the expansion of industrial capitalism in the metropolitan countries depends on the persistence of the pre-capitalist model of production in the peripheral areas (Laclau 1971, 35–7). These ideas were further elaborated by articulation theorists.

Articulation with the Capitalist System

The articulation model differs from the dependency school by virtue of its emphasis on relations of production. Developed by French Marxist anthropologists Pierre-Philippe Rey, Louis Dupré, and Claude Meillassoux, the articulation model tries to explain the survival of subsistence agriculture. The articulation thesis is an elaboration of Marx's concept of "primitive accumulation," which described the transfer of surplus from a feudal to a capitalist economy in a particular historic period, 14th–16th century England. Meillassoux (1981, 105) contends that the "free transfer of values of pre-capitalist societies to imperialist powers is a permanent, and until now an accelerating phenomenon, which has continued to feed the capitalist economy from its outset."

Primitive accumulation, according to Meillassoux, is inherent in the process of the development of the capitalist mode of production (Meillassoux 1981, 105). Surplus accumulation in the capitalist sector is dependent on the wages paid to labour. Since it is cheaper to reproduce labour power inside the domestic economy, it is in the direct interest of the capitalist class to employ migrant labour linked to the subsistence economy. Self-sustaining agriculture and domestic relations of production need to be maintained. Thus, capitalism blocks the development of the pre-capitalist mode of production (Meillassoux 1981, 117).

When migrant labour has access to means of subsistence outside the capitalist sector, the relationship between wages and the cost of production and reproduction of labour is altered. Capital is able to pay the worker below his reproduction cost (Wolpe 1972, 434). For the migrant workers to have access to rural activities, reciprocal kinship obligations have to be reinforced. In South Africa, for instance, several measures were taken by the government, linked to the capitalist sector, to preserve the "tribal" communities (Wolpe 1972, 435–6; Meillassoux 1981, 117).

As stated by Meillassoux (1972, 102), the cheap labour costs come from the super-exploitation, not only of the labour from wage-earner himself, but also of the labour of his kin-group. Thus, lack of the welfare system is compensated for by the traditional rural communities: "By caring for the very young and very old, the sick, the migrant labour in periods of 'rest,' by educating the young, etc., the Reserve families relieve the capitalist sector and its state from the need to expend resources on these necessary functions" (Wolpe 1972, 435).

While originally the articulation approach was developed to explain the persistence of the rural domestic economy, it was further applied to the urban informal economy. Portes (1978, 36) argues that in Latin America these "subsistence transfer strategies" from the agricultural sector do not sufficiently explain the accumulation process in the capitalist sector. He observed that subsistence economies have a diminishing importance in these countries: "For most Latin American countries, it would be risky indeed to affirm that villages producing for subsistence provide the bulk of labour for enterprises in the capitalist sector, or that they fully subsidise its welfare costs." Portes believes that an "additional mechanism" of sustaining effective dominant pressures on labour costs must exist – namely, the informal sector.

ARTICULATION IN THE URBAN ECONOMY

Proponents of the articulation school argue that there are several ways in which accumulation in the capitalist sector is articulated with the informal sector. First, small urban enterprises reduce the need for capitalist firms to provide unemployment insurance for its workers, since the "reserve army of labour" can support itself. Second, they help to keep formal wages down through the provision of some goods and services at a lower cost than can be provided by the formal sector. This allows capitalist employers to pay lower wages (Davies 1979; Lanzetta and Murillo 1989). Third, many inputs purchased by the petty commodity producers come from the capitalist sector. As put by Wellings and Sutcliffe, the "formal sector is in a sense employing the informal sector as a means for entering the lower end of the market" (Wellings and Sutcliffe 1984, 539). Informal sector products are sold to capitalist enterprises at low costs, while capitalist sector products are bought by petty commodity producers at high costs above their value (as a result of monopolist protection, and the fact that the capitalist sector controls access to institutional credit, contracts, and licences). Hence, there are large transfers of value from the urban petty commodity sector to the capitalist sector (Moser 1978; LeBrun and Gerry 1975). Fourth, as LeBrun and Gerry point out, "subordination of petty production to capital can take much more direct forms than those which operate through the market. Certain capitalist enterprises ... sub-contract work on an individual basis thereby reducing the enterprise's production costs" (LeBrun and Gerry 1975, 30). Through subcontracting, the capitalist sector has access to cheap casual labour. The informal labour is adaptable to seasonal demand, allowing formal enterprises to hire and dismiss labour without having to pay unemployment compensation (Portes and Walton 1981, 99).

BENIGN OR MALIGNANT RELATIONS

Even among those who agree about the existence of a complex interaction between capitalist and noncapitalist forms of production, there is disagreement on the exact impact this interaction has on the survival and relative success of small urban enterprises. Some believe that small urban producers occupy a subordinate position in the capitalist economy (Moser 1978) and are likely to be squeezed out in direct competition with the capitalist sector. Others argue that the relations between the two forms of production are mutually functional.

LeBrun and Gerry (1975, 30), for instance, state that "capitalist enterprises have an interest in encouraging the dissolution of petty production which is competitive with their own production." Langdon (1975, 30) argues that in Kenya, multinational corporations (MNCs), through expensive marketing, "establish patterns of demand that are very hard for small-scale indigenous Kenyan industrialists to meet directly. In that sense, the MNC role in Kenya seems responsible for blocking, in a general way, the development of decentralised local industry in a wide range of sectors."

Charmes (1980) compares two occupations in Tunisia: carpentry and mechanical workshops on the one hand, and leather and textiles on the other. While the former is dominated by small producers, the latter has some capitalist enterprises. Carpentry and mechanical workshops are undergoing the process of "conservation," while small leather and textile industries are in the process of "dissolution."

Since petty commodity producers cannot survive in direct competition with capitalist enterprises, some authors (LeBrun and Gerry 1975; Portes and Walton 1981) suggest they are more likely to survive when they stay away from the capitalist-dominated markets and produce only those goods and services that capitalist enterprises do not find profitable. LeBrun and Gerry (1975, 29) contend that capitalist enterprises are oriented towards production of export goods or luxury items for consumption by the elite. Since these enterprises are capital intensive, they employ a small percentage of the urban population. Consequently, their market is also limited. Only petty commodity production is capable of satisfying the largest part of the urban masses' consumption requirements, such as clothing, footwear, housing, furniture, transport, repairs, and cooked food. Portes and Walton (1981, 93) argue that petty commerce is able to counteract the competition presented by large retailing chains because of three conditions: volume of scale, spatial location, and the widespread use of credit. Customers whose income is low and irregular prefer buying in small quantities, which large retail stores do not have available; close to where they live, since transportation costs of shopping at large chain stores may be high; and where credit is available, which cannot be provided by formal businesses.

By forming a niche within the urban economy, by catering to low-income groups, small producers are able to survive. But can they accumulate? Income elasticity of demand for goods and services produced for low-income groups is low (Standing 1977, 43). Hence, even when small enterprise owners can increase production, their sales remain low. Mosley suggests that the sector of the informal economy that caters to a low-income market experiences its greatest stimuli to growth in times of declining real incomes. This growth, however, is involutionary, not evolutionary (Mosley 1978, 9).

In this situation, when existing in an alternative niche means producing for low-income groups, no real possibilities of accumulation exist. However, some activities, not dominated by the capitalist sector, cater to middle- or upper-class clients. These enterprises have

better chances of accumulation as long as the capitalist sector does
not encroach on them.

Articulation theorists argue that relations with the capitalist sector
allow small producers to survive even though they recognize that
informality implies heavy exploitation for the employed labour
(Portes, Castells, and Benton 1989, 300). However, evidence presented by other researchers on the impact of direct relationships
between petty commodity producers and capitalist enterprises is not
clear cut.

Relationships between informal producers and the capitalist sector
can take a number of forms. They include subcontracting work from
capitalist firms by small urban producers, "backward linkages" (purchasing of raw materials and machinery from capitalist enterprises
by petty commodity producers), and "forward linkages" (selling
products and services generated by the noncapitalist sector to capitalist enterprises).

The issue of subcontracting is controversial. Watanabe (1971, 71–
2) argues that subcontracting "can lessen obstacles to small entrepreneurs setting up an enterprise and can help them, once they are
established, to survive and flourish." The ILO Kenya Mission (1972)
suggested that subcontracting should be reinforced. Since then, this
recommendation has become the most common (Senghaas-Knobloch
1977). Souza and Tokman (1976), for instance, proposed establishing
subcontracting "pools" in the private sector by using the state's
purchasing power to buy goods in whose production the informal
sector plays a major part. Bose (1974) argued in the same fashion
that small units can exist only when they allow themselves to be
"exploited" by large units. These recommendations were further
supported by several empirical findings. House (1984, 290) found
that in Nairobi, "far from being exploitative ... linkages with the
formal sector appear to succeed in raising the incomes of subcontract
recipients significantly above those of non-recipients." Van Dijk
(1980) found that in Upper Volta, twenty-five small entrepreneurs
who had capitalist firms as their clients were the most successful
(success was measured in terms of profit, consumption, and number
of employees). By comparison, those workshops that dealt only with
other artisans and small traders demonstrated the worst results.

Schmitz and Gerry challenged the belief that subcontracting is
beneficial to small producers. Schmitz (1982) observed that of the
sample of subcontractors selected from a 1976 register of enterprises

in Brazil, only 50 per cent were still in business in 1979. Gerry's (1978) study of petty commodity producers in Dakar (Senegal) showed that only 2 or 3 per cent of those who linked themselves with large commercial or industrial firms had advanced appreciably. Beneria also draws attention to the dependent nature of small businesses subcontracting from large firms: they can develop only as long as the general development of the country is self-sustaining (Beneria 1989, 185).

The effects of other types of relationships with the capitalist sector on petty commodity producers are equally unclear. There is no conclusive evidence determining whether purchase of raw materials from large capitalist enterprises and sale of products to them are beneficial or exploitative for petty commodity producers.

Gerry (1979) feels that having to buy raw materials from large industries makes it difficult for small producers in Senegal to grow. Yet Schmitz (1982, 32) expresses doubt on the "extent and the way in which this mitigates against the small producers."

Gerry's analysis of the impact of forward linkages on the accumulation process among petty producers does not lead to a single answer. He (1979, 243–4) concludes:

Capital accumulation can equally well occur in a tailoring enterprise which gains a contract to produce prison uniforms, as it can in a tailoring concern producing high-class clothing exclusively for individual clients. The significant factor is not so much for whom one produces, but that one is reasonably assured of a stable and growing clientele or market ... In the case of furniture makers and the metal trades, it appears that involvement with capitalist or State industry gives a certain stability and continuity to production, though it does not necessarily make a significant contribution to increasing incomes.

In sum, some theorists view survival of small urban producers as transitory, as long as they can avoid competition with the capitalist sector. Those who hold the articulation approach believe that informality is a permanent feature of modern capitalism. Furthermore, they argue that relations with capitalist enterprises allow small-scale producers to survive. Yet, there is no clear-cut evidence among other researchers on the impact of relations with the capitalist sector on the survival and success of small enterprises. Chapter 7 addresses this debate by analysing the relative success of small Salvadorean urban enterprises.

7 Relations with the Capitalist Sector

Petty commodity producers, according to some researchers, find it difficult to survive because of competition with the capitalist sector. Other researchers believe that these producers can resist this competition if they follow one of two possible solutions. According to articulation theorists, small urban enterprises survive when they are articulated with the capitalist sector through a variety of mechanisms, including subcontracting from capitalist enterprises, backward linkages (sale of goods or services to them), and forward linkages (purchase of goods from them). The second solution is to create a special economic niche into which capitalist firms have not yet penetrated. What impact do these various relations with the capitalist sector have on relative success among Salvadorean small urban enterprises?

SOCIOECONOMIC CHARACTERISTICS OF SALVADOREANS IN SMALL ENTERPRISES

Since Salvadorean refugees were encouraged to apply for projects of their choice, agency workers did not seem to use any selection criteria, apart from the economic feasibility of the proposed project. Yet it is interesting to analyse how characteristics of Salvadoreans in small businesses compare with those of the Salvadorean community at large in Costa Rica, as reported by Vega (1984) for a sample of 347 Salvadoreans, and by Marmora (1984) for a sample of 1694 Salvadoreans refugees.

Table 16
Age Distribution of Salvadorean Refugees

Age group	Community (out of 347)	Enterprises (out of 156)
	(per cent)	
0–15	0.6	2.6
15–20	15.9	7.1
20–30	38.0	42.3
30–40	23.9	29.5
40–50	5.7	8.3
50–60	10.4	7.7
60 and over	5.8	2.6

Source: Vega (1984)

Comparison of the age distribution of the two populations shows that those between fifteen and twenty years of age and those over sixty are underrepresented in the businesses (see table 16). Many of those over sixty were not integrated into projects, possibly because they were not considered to be economically active by the implementing agencies. Young people (under twenty) had a chance of going to school, while still receiving UNHCR assistance and educational assistance from PRIMAS. The percentage of those under fifteen in business is higher than their percentage in the community as a whole. Three out of four of them were family members of business owners and not project members, and the remaining one was an apprentice. Other age groups were well represented in Salvadorean business. People between twenty and thirty years of age constituted more than one-third in both groups.

In both groups the largest number of refugees had some degree of secondary school education (see table 17). While distribution of Salvadorean refugees in the community is somewhat skewed towards lower levels of education, the distribution of refugees in small businesses is more normal. There are considerably more married people among project participants, other small business owners, and their employees than in the community as a whole (see table 18). This can be explained by underrepresentation of young people among business owners and workers.

Women constituted 31.7 of all Salvadorean refugees (Vega 1984) and made up 32.8 per cent of all refugees working in small businesses. In other words, women were well represented in business.

Table 17
Educational Level of Salvadorean Refugees

Educational level	Community (out of 347)	Enterprises (out of 156)
	(per cent)	
Without schooling	2.6	3.8
Primary school not completed	19.9	15.1
Primary school completed	16.8	18.9
Secondary school not completed	23.9	33.0
Secondary school completed	7.7	21.7
University not completed	10.8	7.6
University completed	1.5	0

Source: Vega (1984)

Table 18
Civil Status of Salvadorean Refugees

Civil status	Community (out of 347)	Enterprises (out of 156)
	(per cent)	
Single	45.2	27.4
Divorced/widowed	6.9	10.9
Married	47.9	61.7

Source: Vega (1984)

People with an industrial background were considerably overrepresented among the refugees in small businesses (see table 19). This training is hardly surprising, given the urban nature of these businesses.

Almost a quarter of all those working in Salvadorean businesses had not been economically active in El Salvador. This proportion corresponds to the situation of the Salvadorean community in general: 27.3 per cent of the Salvadoreans analysed by PRIMAS had been economically inactive in El Salvador (Marmora 1984).

In general, it can be seen that Salvadorean refugees working in projects were representative of Salvadorean refugees in Costa Rica as a whole. Let us now examine relations between these small businesses and the capitalist sector.

SUBCONTRACTING AMONG
SALVADOREAN ENTERPRISES

I found eight Salvadorean producers who were subcontracting. While subcontracting (*maquila*) was chosen as a viable alternative by some

Table 19
Occupational Background of Salvadorean Refugees

Background	Community (out of 347)	Enterprises (out of 156)
	(per cent)	
Industry	29.3	51.6
Agriculture	20.6	14.8
Service	37.7	33.6
No answer	12.2	0.0

Source: Vega (1984)

producers, others were forced into it because they had no choice. One radio and television repair shop, for instance, was poorly located with respect to clients and faced a problem of demand. Its two owners decided to work in a centrally located Costa Rican workshop, using their own tools, and to split their profits evenly with the workshop owner. Although they were losing half their profits, they did not have to pay rent and maintenance costs of the workshop.

Out of five tailoring shops, one was very well equipped and its members had some job-related experience. They chose to subcontract because they thought it was paying off. The other four tailoring shops, however, had to subcontract because their sewing machines could not produce fine, well-finished products, because they lacked the skills to do so, or because their location did not permit a sufficient clientele. Two of these tailoring shops received *maquila* only during the months of high demand (November and December). The remaining two subcontractors were carpenters working in construction. Because they owned tools, they were able to earn more than wage-labourers (*operarios*).

When I compared the incomes of Salvadorean subcontractors to the rest of the Salvadorean enterprise owners, I found that the former, on average, earned 8080 colones while the latter earned 7270 colones per month (n = 72, f-value = 0.17; probability of f > 0.68). In other words, I found no significant difference in income between subcontractors and other producers. Of course, it is difficult to draw conclusions from a sample of eight enterprises, but even within this small group I found a certain degree of heterogeneity. Incomes of subcontractors ranged between 3000 and 20,000 colones per month. Two of them earned between 2000 and 3999 colones monthly, one between 4000 and 5999 colones, one between 6000 and 7999 colones,

Table 20
Monthly Income of Salvadorean Enterprise Owners according to Where Raw Materials Were Purchased

Source of supply of raw materials	No.	Income (colones)
50% or more from capitalist enterprises	40	7,740
Less than 50% from capitalist enterprises	6	4,980
From noncapitalist enterprises	21	7,320

Note: $n = 72$; f-value $= 0.76$; probability of $f > 0.47$

one between 8000 and 9999 colones, one between 10,000 and 11,999 colones, and the remaining two more than 12,000 colones per month. Thus, no clear-cut relation between subcontracting and monthly income seemed to exist.

BACKWARD AND FORWARD LINKAGES AMONG SALVADOREAN ENTERPRISES

For analytical purposes, I divided Salvadorean enterprises into three categories: those that did not buy raw materials from capitalist enterprises;[1] those that purchased less than 50 per cent of raw materials from capitalist enterprises; and those that purchased 50 per cent or more from capitalist enterprises. There seemed to be no significant differences in monthly income among them (see table 20). Basically, there were no differences in monthly income between those that purchased more than 50 per cent of raw materials from capitalist commercial enterprises and those that purchased in the marketplace or from small commercial establishments, because the small Salvadorean enterprises under study did not have a problem of access to raw materials (as was the case in Senegal, discussed by Gerry 1979). The materials were easily available both in small and large commercial enterprises with, possibly, small (if any) differences in price. For certain raw materials it was cheaper to shop at the marketplace and for others, in large department stores. Both were easily accessible and, unless small enterprise owners were poor business administrators, they purchased raw materials where prices were lower. Since most machinery was donated to members of Salvadorean urban enterprises by an agency administering these urban projects, small Salvadorean businesses did not depend on capitalist enterprises for access to machinery.

Only eight Salvadorean enterprises in my sample had forward linkages with the capitalist sector. One was an electro-mechanical repair shop servicing large factories. Its owner was earning over 8000 colones monthly. The other seven enterprises sold their products to large commercial establishments. These enterprises included three bakeries, a candy workshop, two shoe workshops, and one craftsman making bronze-like statuettes. One bakery and the candy workshop sold less than 50 per cent of their products to large supermarkets, whereas the remaining five enterprises sold between 50 and 100 per cent of their products to large commercial establishments.

The monthly income of those who sold to capitalist enterprises ranged between 6000 and 26,000 colones. The average monthly income of those who sold to capitalist enterprises was higher than those who did not (10,400 and 6980 colones, respectively; $n = 72$; f-value $= 3.29$; probability of $f > 0.07$). This possibly reflects the fact that in order to procure contracts from capitalist firms, small enterprises have to be relatively successful – that is, their productivity has to be high enough to satisfy the demand. At the same time, these contracts guarantee stable demand more than do smaller commercial enterprises or markets, thus contributing to a steady source of income. In other words, those producers who obtain contracts from capitalist enterprises are possibly better equipped, hence potentially more successful. Once they establish commercial relations with large enterprises, they are able to earn even more.

COMPETITION OF SALVADOREAN
ENTERPRISES WITH THE CAPITALIST
SECTOR

Salvadorean small enterprises can be divided into three categories on the basis of the degree of competition with capitalist enterprises: those that are outside competition with the capitalist sector because they provide goods or services not offered by large capitalist enterprises; those that, although within the capitalist market, form a separate niche within it; and those that attempt to compete with it.

I used the following criteria to make the distinctions. If a small producer offers a product that is similar to one produced by a capitalist enterprise, they are in competition. A small enterprise is considered to form a separate niche if a product or service is somewhat different but can be replaced by a product or service offered by a capitalist enterprise. And, finally, if a product or service is only produced by small units, they are clearly outside competition with the capitalist sector.

In Costa Rica, there is a division of labour between large shoe factories and artisanal shoemakers. The latter produce women's shoes while the former produce shoes for men and children. While small shoemakers do not face competition from local shoe factories, the same cannot be said about shoe imports. Industrially produced shoes imported from El Salvador or Brazil, for instance,[2] create competition for small producers in Costa Rica. However, there exists a preference among Central American consumers for artisanal shoes, believed to be more comfortable. Thus, small shoemakers offer a type of product different from the industrially produced, and these shoemakers (seven of whom I interviewed) can be said to form a special niche within the capitalist market. Two Salvadoreans in the sample did not receive machinery that would enable them to make shoes and had to offer shoe-repair services instead. Since in Costa Rica this service is limited to small cobblers and there are no chain shoe-repair businesses, the two shoemakers in question were outside competition with the capitalist sector.

Small seamstresses and tailors can also be classified into the three above-mentioned categories – outside competition, forming a niche, or being in competition with the capitalist sector. Clothes repairers offer a service not available through the formal sector and are therefore outside competition with it. Clothing manufacturers can be placed in the other two categories according to what type of clothes they produce. When they make custom-made clothes they offer a special product to a client and form a niche within the market. When the clothes they produce are standard and are sold not to individual customers but to stores or in the streets, the seamstresses and tailors are competing with clothes manufacturing factories. Among Salvadorean enterprises in my sample, there was one seamstress repairing clothes ("outside" competition), ten textile workshops producing custom-made clothes (forming a niche), and four textile workshops that were in competition with the capitalist sector since they produced standard clothes.

Bakeries, although competing with industries, produce a different kind of bread and can be said to occupy a separate niche. There were ten such bakeries among the Salvadoreans under study. One other

Salvadorean bakery entered into direct competition with a large factory – La Selecta – since the two enterprises produced similar pastries.

Similar to bakeries, small restaurants (*sodas*) offer different food from such chain restaurants as McDonald's, Pizza Hut, Kentucky Fried Chicken, or Antojitos. The former produce home-made dishes (*comida casera*), which include such traditional dishes as *gallo pinto* (rice and beans) and *casado* (a mixture of stewed beef, rice, fried plantains, eggs, home fries, and black beans). These *sodas*, five of which were found among the Salvadoreans, form a special niche.

Two Salvadorean street vendors who prepared and sold snacks, such as *pupusas* (Salvadorean stuffed tortillas) or *empanadas* (patties), were outside competition with the formal sector. So, also, were those Salvadorean enterprises that offered personal services, such as one hairdresser, two photographers, and a house painter. A car painter, however, faced competition from such large enterprises as Lachner y Saenz, Romero y Fournier, and Carrocería 3R.

Carpenters can sell finished products to private customers, as did two Salvadorean shops, thus forming a niche; or they can sell to stores or large institutions, as did one carpentry shop, thus competing with industrial furniture factories. The only leather goods producer in my sample made leather goods similar to those produced by capitalist enterprises, and therefore was in competition with them.

Those who offer mechanical and electro-mechanical repairs are usually outside competition with the capitalist sector, as were four Salvadorean workshops. One automechanic, however, was competing with capitalist autorepair shops, such as Lachner y Saenz, Romero y Fournier, and Carrocería 3R.

There were five handicrafts shops among Salvadoreans under study, including two workshops painting wooden jewel boxes in the traditional Salvadorean style *La Palma*, one shop making handwoven fabrics, one hammock-maker, and one bronze-like statuette maker. They made their products by hand or used simple technology, so their products differed from industrially produced crafts. Yet many tourists buying souvenirs in Costa Rica do not necessarily prefer Salvadorean painted boxes over those produced by a Costa Rican factory Sol y Sol, for instance. The same can be said about hammocks or statuettes. The handicrafts, although different from industrially produced souvenirs, could nevertheless be substituted by them.

Handicraftsmen, therefore, formed a special niche within the capitalist market.

Small food stores (*pulperías*) compete with supermarkets. Their location, however, makes them an alternative to shopping in supermarkets for residents of the barrio. They therefore form a niche, as did one Salvadorean food store. Clothing stores are in competition with large department stores. People do not buy clothes every day and they usually prefer shopping for clothes where they are cheaper and/or of better quality, and not just because a clothing store is conveniently located in their neighbourhood. One Salvadorean clothing store was in this category. Nonfood street vendors (there was one jewel vendor among the Salvadoreans) are in competition with the capitalist sector.

My sample of Salvadorean enterprises also included a candy workshop, a soapmaker, and a tinsmith. The soapmaker was in competition with the capitalist sector because the soap he made was similar to *jabon azul*, industrially made soap. The candy shop and the tinsmith, in contrast, offered products that were of inferior quality to those industrially produced. Candies produced in this shop, for instance, had no wrapping, and eavesdrops made by the tinsmith used poor-quality aluminum. By catering to low-income clientele who could afford their goods, these producers formed a niche within the capitalist market.

To summarize, small enterprises in competition with the capitalist sector included four clothes producers, a bakery, a car painter, a carpentry shop, a leather production shop, an auto mechanic, a clothing store, a jewel vendor, and a small soapmaker (see table 21). The small enterprises that occupied a special niche within the capitalist market consisted of seven shoe-producing workshops, ten small clothes manufacturing shops, ten bakeries, five restaurants, two carpentry shops, five handicrafts shops, a food store, a tinsmith, and a candy shop. Finally, those outside the capitalist market included two cobblers, a seamstress repairing clothes, two street snack vendors, a beauty salon, two photographers, a painter, two watch repairers, one electrician, and an electrical mechanic.

I expected to find that those enterprises outside the capitalist market would be more successful than those forming a special niche within it, and that small producers in both of these categories would be earning more than those trying to compete with the capitalist

Table 21
Small Salvadorean Enterprises according to Type of Relationship with the Capitalist Sector
by Occupation

Occupation	Outside	Niche	Compete	Total
Shoe-making	2	7	0	9
Clothes-making/				
repair	1	10	4	15
Bakery	0	10	1	11
Food production	2	5	0	7
Personal services	4	0	1	5
Carpentry	0	2	1	3
Leather goods	0	0	1	1
Production				
repairs	4	0	1	5
Crafts production	0	5	0	5
Commerce	0	1	2	3
Other	0	2	1	3
Total	13	42	12	67

sector. However, when I compared average incomes of the producers in the three categories, it became clear that there were no significant differences among them, although those enterprise owners who attempted to compete with the capitalist sector did earn somewhat less (see table 22). There does not seem to be a simple association between relative success of small businesses and relations with the capitalist sector, as far as competition between the two sectors is concerned.

Furthermore, it is interesting to note that each category of relation to the capitalist sector demonstrated a wide range of incomes (see table 23). In addition, comparison of income distribution within each of these categories shows no major differences: 62 per cent of those outside competition in comparison to 58 per cent of those in competition with the capitalist sector earned less than 6000 colones monthly. In fact, there are proportionately more producers earning less than 4000 per month among those who were outside competition than those who formed a special niche or who were in direct competition with the capitalist sector (54 per cent, 31 per cent, and 25 per cent, respectively).

The analysis of small Salvadorean enterprises in terms of their relations with the capitalist sector indicated no major differences in

Table 22
Average Monthly Income by Type of Relationship to the Capitalist Sector

Relation	Income (colones)
Outside	7,370
Niche	7,400
Compete	6,660

Note: n = 64; f-value = 0.07; probability of f > 0.93

Table 23
Monthly Income Levels according to Type of Relationship with the Capitalist Sector

Income levels	Outside	Niche	Compete	Total
		(frequency)		
Less than 2,000	3	3	1	7
2,000–3,999	4	10	2	16
4,000–5,999	1	6	4	11
6,000–7,999	1	7	1	9
8,000–9,999	2	6	0	8
10,000–11,999	0	4	0	4
More than 12,000	2	6	4	12
Total	13	42	12	67

average monthly incomes (which was taken as a measure of relative success). Only small enterprises that sold their products or services to capitalist factories or commercial establishments were found to have higher incomes in relation to those who sold to small stores or private customers. But even in their case, it was not clear whether enterprises that procured contracts from capitalist enterprises had been potentially more successful or whether their businesses grew because of these contracts. The most likely answer is that both explanations are valid.

Those producers who purchased raw materials from large commercial enterprises did as well as those who bought supplies in small stores. In urban Costa Rica, small producers of the type analysed in this study do not have problems procuring raw materials from either small or large enterprises.

With respect to subcontracting, no single explanation can be provided. While for some producers subcontracting offered a better solution in relation to other alternatives, for others subcontracting was the only opportunity for survival (even if it meant only temporary relief), given inadequacies of machinery, skills, and/or location.

The type of relation with the capitalist sector did not seem to account for the variability of income among the small enterprises under study. However, this conclusion should be viewed with a certain degree of caution: because of the unequal distribution of enterprises among the categories corresponding to different types of relations they had with the capitalist sector, statistical analysis is not powerful. In spite of this limitation, the data clearly point out the heterogeneity among small urban producers, which cannot be explained by the nature of their relations with capitalist enterprises. This conclusion corresponds to the lack of clear-cut evidence on the impact of these relations on economic survival, and the success of petty commodity producers in the countries studied by other researchers (see chapter 6).

8 Internal Aspects of Production

If the type of relations small urban enterprises have with the capitalist sector does not explain their relative success, what does? Both the petty commodity production and the articulation approaches place emphasis on external relations or those relations formed when the product or service are marketed. These approaches largely ignore internal aspects of production, including means of production and productive relations.

As Blincow contends, an analysis of petty commodity producers "must concentrate on the specifics of the domain of production as the essential locus within which the process of transformation occurs" (Blincow 1986, 114). Friedmann (1986, 119–20) relates this issue to what she calls the "problem of totality," by which she means the mistake of assuming that "everything is capitalist in the 'capitalist world system.'" Thus, by regarding the petty commodity form of production only from the point of view of its relations with the capitalist sector, these theorists largely ignore the internal dynamic of petty commodity production as a different form of production. By doing so, they "draw the false conclusion that existing social formations are a product of an adaptation to rather than a struggle against, this single, overriding capitalist rationality," as stated by Kahn (1986, 52). Thus, what is needed is an analysis of petty commodity producers' means, relations, and organization of production.

MEANS OF PRODUCTION

Means of production include technology, workers with their skills and knowledge, and raw materials. As demonstrated in chapter 5, the possession of adequate machinery by Salvadorean small producers had a definite impact on their income. Salvadorean women were often underequipped. Most of the interviewed women received a type of assistance from nongovernmental organizations (NGOs) that only allowed them to sew clothes or bake bread and pastries at home using domestic machinery. Seamstresses were given sewing machines that did not allow them to finish their product well, with the result that the clothes they produced were of inferior quality and could only be sold for low prices. Bread and pastry makers were given regular stoves that consumed a large amount of energy and required much time for cooking, thus making production extremely inefficient. While there is a danger of underequipping small producers, there is also a danger of overequipping them. Often limitations in demand for goods produced by small enterprises do not justify high investments in machinery. Among several Salvadoreans producers, semi-industrial technology donated by NGOs was underutilized. If workshop owners had to purchase this machinery on credit at a commercial bank rate, their incomes would have been negative.

Lack of technical skills among small-scale producers also affected their incomes. Salvadorean women were especially disadvantaged in this regard. NGOs offering assistance to Salvadorean refugees assumed that every woman knew how to sew and bake. However, repairing and making clothes or baking pastries for household use is not the same as producing commercial goods. Yet most of these women were not offered any training in commercial production. Those women who were sent to the National Institute for Training to take a baking course learned to bake homemade cookies, not a useful skill for commercial baking.

Additionally, refugees lacked administrative skills to manage projects. In 1983 Caritas started offering three-day business administration courses. However, most informants felt that these courses were too short to teach them adequate skills.

Purchase of raw materials without access to credit presented another problem. Many refugees had to sell their goods and/or services on credit, yet they did not enjoy credit from other lending or commercial institutions. Consequently, they had to purchase raw materials in small quantities and were not able to take advantage of lower prices for bulk goods. When business was slow, they could not purchase raw materials to produce more goods at all.

INSTITUTIONAL PATERNALISM

When discussing relations of production it is useful to distinguish between those that were imposed upon Salvadorean producers by agencies in charge of the projects and those they themselves established. The former created obstacles for Salvadorean informal producers; the latter were used as strategies of survival.

Even though Salvadorean refugees were told they were owners of their businesses, some agencies held a legal title to the equipment provided for the business and continued to interfere with production decisions made by project members. Because of the paternalistic attitude assumed by some agencies, project beneficiaries felt they were merely wage-labourers working for a boss – the agency.

Agencies administering projects differed in their attitude towards project members. There were some agencies (like Caritas, PRIMAS, and the YMCA) that practised a paternalistic approach to their members. Other agencies (such as the Episcopalian church, OARS, and Productor) allowed refugees to develop independently, although still controlling some of their decisions and at times offering more help to them than was required.

In 1985, when an evaluation of projects was conducted by the Caritas technical team (Jimenez 1985), one of the reasons for failure was a "limited sense of belonging to a project" among the members. According to this report, participants maintained interest exclusively in earning a salary and, when the slightest opportunity arose, they left projects "without a minimal resistance." There was also a "certain lack of trust" (*disconfianza*) by refugees towards the Caritas technical assistance team, which was regarded as an "external agent" operating on its own interest.

Refugees' failure to identify themselves with the projects can be explained. Relations between Caritas and project members were defined in the Caritas constitution (*Reglamento*) as a set of rights and obligations. The obligations incumbent upon the project members included presenting monthly financial statements to the technical team, informing it of any changes having to do with the employment of new members or withdrawal of the original ones, and of the socioeconomic situation of the beneficiaries and their economic activities. Members were not allowed to take personal loans from the money belonging to the enterprise. Refugees were obliged to provide information when Caritas or any other group evaluated the projects. They were to stay away from political or religious activities that could interfere with the economic life of their workshop. Caritas had the right unilaterally to expel any member who did not comply with the rules. Machinery given to the projects was always the property of the agency and, at any moment, could be taken away from the refugees.

All projects were under Caritas control even five years after they were established. When a workshop moved to another location, members were obliged to call the office and provide their new address. If they failed to do so, Caritas officials called the Department of Immigration to advise them to discontinue all types of assistance to which the refugees in question were eligible.

Salvadoreans were placed in the position of wage-labourers under the control of one employer – Caritas. Some of the interviewed project members reported having been told by Caritas that they were just wage-labourers (*operarios*). When asked about the ownership of machinery, most of the informants did not know to whom it belonged. They felt that Caritas was still in control and were afraid that one day they would lose it.

Most Salvadoreans viewed Caritas as promoting its own interests and not being concerned about the refugees. In fact, there was a shared opinion among them that because Caritas wanted projects to fail, its workers would take away the machinery. In some cases, Caritas was accused of instigating the conflicts among project members. Stories about a warehouse full of machinery confiscated from workshops that had closed down or where some members had left were often mentioned in the interviews. Whether such a warehouse existed is irrelevant. What is important is that most of the refugees believed it did exist and that this was partly the cause of their negative attitude towards the agency.

Caritas was also often accused of embezzling funds given by UNHCR. Those who did not accuse Caritas of theft believed that the only reason it promoted projects for refugees was so UNHCR would pay its administrative costs. In fact, Caritas did seem to retain a large percentage of refugee funds. According to an ILO agent, who prepared a report on Caritas, the agency's administrative cost constituted 33.3 per cent of $1,217,759 donated by the UNHCR between 1981 and 1985. Even in comparison with other refugee project implementing agencies, the percentage was high.

Many informants had their stories to tell about Caritas. One woman who was the only survivor of a ten-person project had all her machinery confiscated by Caritas. Members of another project were forced to buy raw materials left over from the workshops that had closed down. As they discovered later, they had paid three times the price of what they could have paid elsewhere. Some people were asked to sign blank cheques by Caritas employees. When they refused, the project was closed. It was felt by some refugees that while international agencies were interested in aiding them, the Costa Ricans working at Caritas tried harming them in order to protect the national labour force.

Other implementing agencies, such as OARS, Productor, and the Episcopalian church, did not seem to be paternalistic in their relations with the refugees. The Episcopalian church offered more freedom to project members than did Caritas. Its administrative costs constituted 7 per cent of the total donation per project. Beneficiaries were asked to sign a contract that stated if, in two years, a project proved to be self-sufficient, all the fixed and fluid capital was to become their property. If self-sufficiency was not reached, the Episcopalian church had the right to claim back the machinery to be used in other projects. The terms of the contract were observed and, two years after implementation, successful projects were completely "liberated." The Episcopalian church workers were often unaware of the new location of these liberated projects. When these enterprises were visited, it was out of personal interest and not in order to interfere with the projects' affairs.

Although, in comparison with Caritas, the relations between the Episcopalian church and the refugees were considerably better, project participants did, nevertheless, express some complaints about this agency. One workshop that was doing rather poorly was threatened with closure by the representatives of the Episcopalian church. Although this would have been in agreement with the terms of contract between the project and the agency, Salvadoreans working in it felt they deserved a chance to keep on struggling for their survival, even though it meant earning a very low income. It is the nature of most implementing agencies to be economically "rational." Although the above-mentioned project was not economically feasible, its members felt they were fulfilling an important political and cultural role by promoting a Salvadorean traditional craft (handwoven fabrics).

Since most of the OARS and Productor staff members were themselves Salvadorean refugees, they had a good rapport with project participants. However, these two agencies viewed projects as solutions to all refugee problems. They paid more attention to the refugees' social and psychological needs than to the economic aspects of the enterprise. This emphasis may have enhanced refugee/agency relations, but it consumed resources and energy that might otherwise have been used to strengthen the economic side of the project.

The Episcopalian church was also concerned with the socio-psychological well-being of refugees. They tried to address this problem by organizing retreat-like workshops (*convivencias*) at which refugees were asked to share their experience of life and persecution in El Salvador, as well as difficulties of their emigration and their life in Costa Rica. All employees of the Episcopalian church participated in these seminars, along with some Costa Rican priests. They ate and prayed together. At the same time, the Episcopalian church workers tried not to ignore the economic performance of projects administered by them.

Why does it matter whether refugees in projects are treated paternalisticly? In *Economic and Philosophic Manuscripts*, Marx drew attention to the alienation of wage labour. Alienated workers do not affirm but deny themselves and therefore feel unhappy. Their labour is not voluntary but is coerced and it gives them no satisfaction; it is labour of self-sacrifice, of mortification (Marx 1964, 110–11). When refugees felt that means of production and productive decisions were controlled by agencies in charge of implementing the projects, they felt alienated and therefore were not motivated to work hard. Those refugees who owned their projects (*de facto* and *de jure*) usually made every effort to make their businesses succeed.

It is important to mention another problem associated with paternalistic control on the part of agencies implementing projects. Agency workers are often not very knowledgeable in how to conduct a particular business, yet they impose their advice, which is at best useless and at worst harmful.

Some shoemakers complained to me about the Caritas team of "experts" who came to give them advice. The "experts" knew nothing about making shoes and could not offer any useful advice to the shoemakers, who had been in the business for many years (one of them had owned a shoe workshop employing ten people in El Salvador). Some advice was against the economic interests of the project members. Caritas advisers, for instance, insisted that seamstresses and tailors should sell their products to stores, arguing that this arrangement guaranteed a stable market to producers. While the recommendation was valid for group projects, individual seamstresses and tailors did much better catering to private customers. Stores pay considerably less than private customers, because they need to leave room for their own profit margin and because they can purchase industrially produced textiles for relatively low prices. In the words of one tailor, when he sold to stores, he was "working too much for too little." In another instance, a two-man TV and radio repair project had a poor location and the men worked in a centrally located Costa Rican workshop, using their own tools and sharing profits with the workshop owner. Though that seemed to be the only viable solution to them, Caritas consistently opposed it.

It is often important in business to take a risk. It may result in the downfall of the business or it may allow it to prosper. Agencies offering assistance tend to be cautious in their decisions and, by doing so, they sometimes slow down the development of an enterprise. Participants of one project administered by the Episcopalian church complained that their entrepreneurial freedom was blocked by the agency and that it was only after their liberation that their business began to develop rapidly.

As can be seen, these complaints do not have to do with special policies of the Episcopalian church as much as with problems involved in the relation between institutions in general and individuals depending on them. The sooner this relation is severed, the better it may be for a project.

COLLECTIVE OWNERSHIP

Advantages and disadvantages of cooperative versus individual ownership of production are widely debated in development sociology

(Dumont 1969; Lappe and Collins 1986, 72–6; Ghose 1983, for instance). Whenever people are forced to collectivize (as they were in Eastern Europe, Peru, Cuba, and other countries), they seem to lack interest in communal production. This was the problem with many Salvadorean urban projects.

Most of the projects implemented through the durable solution program were of a collective nature, some including as many as twenty members and one project including forty members. The first reason for this arrangement had to do with economics – namely, centralizing administrative and technical assistance, increasing competitiveness, and purchasing large quantities of raw materials. The second reason was linked to the policy of international funding agencies, which promoted collective projects. And third, Salvadorean implementing agencies hoped that by promoting group projects they would be able to unite the Salvadorean community. They also believed that once trained to work in cooperatives, Salvadoreans would be able to do the same on their return to their homeland. Moreover, it was believed that working in a group project would be a kind of therapy for those refugees who had psychological problems.

Two problems arose because of this policy. First, while business management skills are less important in individual projects, they are essential in collective projects. Very few Salvadorean refugees had those skills. Second, interpersonal conflicts often arose and led to withdrawal by some members or closure of the project.

Before September 1982, refugees were responsible for forming the group and choosing the type of project in which they wished to participate. Some of these people had a desire to work in a chosen field but had no labour experience in it. In September 1982, however, agencies began to direct refugees to particular projects. As a result, people who had been strangers to each other had to work side by side. They were all told they had equal rights and, as a consequence, no one wanted to take orders, thus creating virtual anarchy in projects. Conflicts were also provoked because some people, who had more skills than others, demanded higher pay. Finally, people with different political views were often forced to work together. Political disputes interfered with their working relations.

Despite these problems, agencies continued to promote projects of medium and large size. This policy was also supported by independent consultants who evaluated projects for refugees in Costa Rica. An ILO researcher, for instance, contended that "the very concept of promoting primarily small projects is the cause of their failure" (Marmora 1984, 83). These projects, for instance, had problems in marketing their products, since they could not generate an economy of scale. By creating small projects, implementing agencies were increasing activities among the urban informal sector, which was already saturated, and refugee projects were creating competition to the local labour force (Marmora 1984, 84, 90). The Costa Rican informal sector was not saturated, however, and national small-scale producers were not threatened by competition from Salvadorean small enterprises. In fact, if Salvadorean projects had been larger than ten participants and could have benefited from the economy of scale, they would have created more competition for Costa Rican small producers.

STRATEGIES OF SURVIVAL: AN IMPORTANT DIMENSION

So far in this study, refugees have been viewed as victims first of competition with the capitalist sector and then of paternalistic and incorrect policies adopted by agencies implementing their projects. However, refugees (just like any other small producers) are not simply victims; they are actors in the process. When faced with adverse conditions they employ certain strategies of survival that make them resilient.

The concept of strategies of survival was first used by Duque and Pastrana (1973) as an explanation of survival by poor families. These authors emphasized the economic aspects of survival or the reorganization of family functions in such a way that all, or a majority of, its members participated in procuring income. This concept was further elaborated by a team of researchers working at PISPAL (1978) who, in addition to material reproduction, included biological reproduction in the discussion of survival.

Still other researchers broadened the concept by adding social and cultural aspects of behaviour, as well as the context in which these strategies take place. Survival strategies were defined by Arguello (1981, 197) as

a combination of economic, social, cultural and demographic actions employed by those strata of population who have neither sufficient means of production nor full-time employment in the labour market, and who for that reason do not have regular income to support their existence at a socially determined level, given structural problems of the predominant style of development.

Along with emphasis on the marginal[1] position of people adopting such behaviour vis-à-vis the predominant labour market (Rodriguez 1981, 240; Arguello 1981, 195), a discussion of the "threat" to their material and biological reproduction (Valdes and Acuña 1981) was linked with the concept of strategies of survival.

Although the notion of strategies of survival is usually applied to families, it can also be used with respect to informal enterprises. Small businesses are usually found in unfavourable conditions where their participation in institutional credit, government tax shelters, subsidies, and other benefits is very restricted or marginal. Their existence is threatened by competition coming from the capitalist sector. As a consequence, these small enterprises adopt certain strategies of survival that allow them to survive in spite of these disadvantages (McGee 1974; Smart 1988).

There are two problems associated with the concept of strategies of survival. First, the notion of strategy implies a certain rationality – the calculation of objectives, ends, means, and results by people involved in this behaviour. Whether such rationality exists in all cases is not always clear (Torrado 1981, 206, 212). Second, the notion of survival implies that this concept applies exclusively to those types of behavior related to minimal subsistence levels, thus restricting its application only to the most disadvantaged groups of people (Torrado 1981, 206). However, as Arguello (1981) argues, these strategies can be employed not by the marginalized, underemployed people, but also by the urban and rural petty bourgeoisie. These two limitations should be borne in mind in a discussion of the concept of strategies of survival.

Strategies of survival include specific relations of production and organization of production. Relations of production are characterized by exploitation of the labour of apprentices, employment of household labour in production and marketing, reliance on friendship ties, and self-exploitation.

Hiring Apprentices

Because informal enterprises are not subject to labour legislation, their owners tend to exploit labour employed in them. Apprentices

Table 24
Comparison of Incomes of Salvadorean Enterprise Owners and Apprentices

Case no.	Average incomes of owners adjusted to 45 hours	Average incomes of apprentices adjusted to 45 hours
1	11,300	6,300
2	5,300	3,400
3	8,500	8,500
4	6,250	1,880
5	13,450	8,000
6	3,150	2,150
7	7,350	3,100
8	6,750	6,750
9	13,000	2,700
10	12,000	9,000

face the hardest working conditions (Leonard 1980; Miras 1980; Charmes 1980).

Ten Salvadorean small businesses in my study hired apprentices. However, these apprentices were not exploited as much as other apprentices reported elsewhere. In fact, in two cases, apprentices were earning as much as project members (see table 24). In the first case (no. 3), two apprentices were placed in the business along with two project members by the agency that implemented the project, and the salary may have been a reflection of the institutional policy vis-à-vis the apprentices. In the second case (no. 8), the apprentice was a brother of one of the owners, and kinship obligations, rather than economic rationality in a strict sense, must have influenced his salary. In the remaining cases, on average, apprentices earned approximately one-half (52 per cent) of the salary of project members. Although not great, a difference in income between owners and apprentices did exist and employment of apprentices probably allowed project owners to save money. A better discussion of this issue would have been possible if the productivity of apprentices had been calculated and compared with that of wage-labourers and owners. This, unfortunately, was not done in the study.

Employment of Household Labour

Along with apprentices, household members provide cheap (or free) labour, allowing the enterprise to cut down on costs of production.

Additionally, hiring family members makes it easier to manage the business (Tangri 1982; Peattie 1982; Buechler 1982).

Seven Salvadorean project owners in my study used unpaid family labour. Wives worked in four of them and children in the remaining three. In one case a wife worked thirty-six hours per week. In the other businesses, family members worked sporadically. By comparison, paid family labour was used in eighteen Salvadorean small businesses. Given that interpersonal problems were frequent in Salvadorean projects and at times led to their closing down, it was advantageous to place members of the same household in the project since the latter were less likely to fight. All family members were paid a salary in these cases as they were equal members of the project. Placing both spouses (and perhaps also their children) in the same project could only be done if both of them had, or could easily learn, the skills necessary for the job. As can be seen, the importance of employment of family labour within Salvadorean small businesses lies not merely in the economic sphere (saving on salary) but also in the sphere of social relations.

Social Networks as Channels for Marketing and Advertising

Friendship and kinship networks can be instrumental to the survival of informal enterprises insofar as they provide them with free venues for advertising and marketing (Long and Richardson 1978; LeBrun and Gerry 1975; Kennedy 1981). Social networks played a significant role in the survival and success of small Salvadorean businesses. Four projects reported relying on Salvadorean friends only in finding clientele, fourteen projects used non-Salvadorean friends for this purpose, and ten used both. Friendships were useful in other areas as well. For instance, four small producers used their friends' sewing machines, and in two cases Salvadorean seamstresses purchased fabrics from their friends who worked in textile factories and who were given a considerable discount.

Given that evangelical groups form a religious minority in Central America, social ties among them seem to be especially strong. One Salvadorean baker, for instance, lived with a Costa Rican evangelical family who charged her no rent and, in addition, allowed her to use their stove for baking. Another member purchased some sewing machines on credit from a shopowner of his religious persuasion. Still another seamstress, a wife of an evangelical pastor, sold clothing to members of her congregation.

Friendship ties with foreigners were also beneficial for Salvadorean business owners. One lady was given a present of an oven and another a sewing machine by American friends.

Self-Exploitation

Another characteristic of informal producers is self-exploitation through working long hours and working inside one's home (Gerry 1979; Ybarra 1989). Owners of thirty-one small Salvadorean enterprises worked more than forty-five hours, some as many as seventy per week. In terms of the immediate success of an enterprise it is beneficial to work longer hours, but in the long run this practice may result in rapid personal decline.

It is also common for small enterprise owners to work at home, thus saving on rent but possibly polluting their residential environment. This was the case for fifty-one Salvadorean small enterprises.

SUBCONTRACTING TO OTHER SMALL PRODUCERS

Earlier, subcontracting by small producers from large capitalist enterprises was discussed as a means of survival. The same process occurs among the small producers themselves and allows for differentiation among them. In my study, I found two Salvadoreans who were subcontracting to other small producers. One was a seamstress and the other a tailor. They employed subcontractors who worked at home, using their own machinery. Both small producers had successful businesses (one making 20,000 colones and the other 14,000 colones per month). In both cases they first had to establish clientele, and only when demand became greater than their ability to produce did they hire subcontractors. This condition of demand having to outweigh supply restricts most other Salvadoreans from employing subcontractors, since they have a balance between demand and supply or the latter is greater than the former.

ADVANTAGES OF SMALL-SCALE
PRODUCTION

It is often argued that medium- and large-scale enterprises have an advantage of the economy of scale that permits concentration of resources, more efficient exploitation of machinery, and easier and cheaper marketing. Yet small-scale enterprises offer certain advantages as well. First, they are more adaptable to changes in demand (MacEwan Scott 1979; Long and Richardson 1978; Schmitz 1982). Second, in times of financial crises they allow their owners to oscillate between various income-earning activities without abandoning the enterprise (Hart 1973; Long and Richardson 1978; Standing 1977; Schmitz 1982).

Salvadorean small enterprises producing custom-made products are by their nature adaptable to demand. However, even when small producers make standard clothes, they can still allow for some variations related to the customer's taste. One seamstress narrated:

I don't like making custom-made clothes because some customers end up not liking the product and then I cannot sell it to anyone else anymore. I usually make standard clothes and then take them to an office where a friend of mine works. Some ladies see the dresses I make and say "If the dress was of a different colour, I would buy it" or "If it was one size bigger I would like it." Then I go home and make a similar dress but of the colour they want or the size they need.

Salvadorean petty commodity producers, especially craftsmen, revealed considerable creativity and inventiveness in the face of competition or other problems. One Salvadorean craftsman making small painted boxes changed his designs completely (thus deviating from the traditional Salvadorean wood-painting school called La Palma) when he faced too much competition from other Salvadorean craftsmen.

The creativity and adaptability is found not only in the product but also in materials small producers use. One artisan, for instance, invented a mix that considerably lowered his production costs in making bronze-like statuettes. One shoe repairer managed to buy leather wastes, which he used to make heels.

With respect to diversification of income-generating activities, I found that members of sixteen small Salvadorean enterprises combined work in their business with other employment. Reasons for doing so were various:

- Four business owners selling ethnic products or catering to the ethnic clientele faced a problem of insufficient demand.
- Three other small entrepreneurs also had low demand for their services, but in their case it was because all these businesses had recently opened.
- The problems of seasonal demand affected the owner of a *soda*, located at the National University. He could work in his enterprise only during the academic year. During the months of summer vacation the demand was so low that he preferred working as a gardener for wages.
- Four Salvadoreans had inadequate machinery, which allowed them to perform only a limited number of operations and put certain restrictions on production. One of them, a shoemaker, worked in a Costa Rican shoe shop where he could use some machinery to produce shoes for his own business.
- Two business owners supplemented their income by working in other jobs so they could pay off personal debts they had incurred in order to expand their enterprises.
- The remaining Salvadoreans took additional jobs simply to earn more money.

Members of four of these small businesses worked for wages in the same occupation as their own enterprises, four for wages in other occupations, three picked coffee during the harvest, and five had other small businesses. Refugees working for wages wanted to maintain their own enterprises for the sake of independence, which they would be able to enjoy if and when the business grew, and also because the wage jobs were illegal and could be lost at any time. It is worth examining why the secondary enterprises had not become the major sources of income for these refugees. Analysis of the five cases where refugees owned several enterprises shows that the secondary businesses faced a limited demand and could serve only as an additional source of income.

The case of Doña Santos provides a vivid illustration of the link between diversification and survival. Doña Santos is a single mother supporting two children who have a mental disability. She received a small sewing machine from CASP/Re. She and her Costa Rican neighbour both use this machine to make dresses that Doña Santos sells door to door. Several years ago she learned to make Christmas decorations. She makes them all through the year and sells them to Lehmans, a large department store. She is paid only once a year, after Christmas. Whatever is not sold is returned to her. This year she managed to get a permit to put up a stall at a bus terminal. She hired a Costa Rican boy to sell the decorations. During the coffee harvest she picks coffee as well. She could not survive on making clothes alone since the sewing machine she received yields low-quality products and has low productivity. At the same time, both coffee picking and sales of Christmas decorations are seasonal.

WEAK SEPARATION BETWEEN
PRODUCTION AND HOUSEHOLD

Informal businesses have another organizational advantage: household income is weakly separated from business needs (Hart 1973; Long and Richardson 1978; Schmitz 1982; Peattie 1982). Salvadorean households gave material support to small producers who were doing badly. Ten female business owners relied on their husbands' salaries to maintain their workshops; three other women and five single men had the support of their parents. It seems that financial support from other members of the household was important for the physical survival of small producers but not their businesses. All the males who relied on assistance from household members belonged to collective projects and did not invest money earned by other household members into their enterprises. The women, in contrast, formed individual enterprises, but all of them earned so little (less than 4500 colones per month) that, even if they did use money earned by other household members, these transfers were possibly done only occasionally. In other words, there were no systematic transfers of money earned by some household members into businesses operated by other household members among the Salvadoreans. Yet the material support from household members played a role in the survival (but not the success) of small enterprises, since it prevented their owners from abandoning these businesses to find employment in more profitable but, possibly, less secure occupations.

CONCLUSION

In order to understand why small urban enterprises are viable in spite of constraints imposed by competition with the capitalist sector, it is important to analyse some internal aspects of these businesses, including the means, relations, and organization of production. It is also necessary to distinguish between those relations of production that are imposed on them by agencies providing them with assistance and those they themselves choose to have. Thus, both paternalism on the part of refugee assisting agencies and the policy of creating collective enterprises were detrimental to small Salvadorean producers. At the same time, many small producers organized their production in such a way as to become to resilient.

Conclusion

THEORETICAL IMPLICATIONS OF THE STUDY

Survival and re-emergence of precapitalist forms of production among the so-called informal enterpreneurs in the capitalist economy have presented a challenge to those scholars of development who believe in the unilinear process of modernization. There have been several attempts to explain these phenomena. Some theorists believe that precapitalist forms of production are going through both conservation and dissolution. Conservation is possible when informal producers avoid competition with the capitalist sector by creating a special niche for themselves in the economic market. Dissolution occurs when capitalist production expands into these niches. These theorists believe that persistence of petty commodity production is a temporary phenomenon; it is possible only as long as there are still some economic areas into which capitalist firms have not penetrated.

By contrast, articulation theorists view informal petty commodity production as a significant part of the modern capitalist economy. They argue that informal enterprises survive by being functional to the process of accumulation of capital in the industrial sector. Although different, the two approaches share emphasis on relations with the capitalist sector in explaining the economic survival and success of petty commodity producers.

The study of Salvadorean urban enterprise owners pointed out that neither the competition avoidance nor the articulation approach accounts for variability in success of small producers. Even those small producers who had similar relations with the capitalist sector varied considerably in income levels. Those most exploited by the capitalist sector (through subcontracting) at times earned a good living.

These conclusions should be viewed with a certain degree of caution. First, because of the unequal distribution of producers among the categories corresponding to different types of relations with the capitalist sector, a statistical analysis is not reliable. Second, the study analysed direct, but not indirect relations with the capitalist sector. Indirect relations, for example, refer to the role of petty commodity producers in keeping industrial wages down. As Lanzetta and Murillo (1989, 109) point out:

In contrast with those studies that have emphasized the significance of subcontracting, our results are interpretable as highlighting the significance of a second mode of articulation with the formal economy, namely, that in which informal activities play a central role in facilitating the reproduction of the urban working class by providing, simultaneously, access to (casual) income sources and to low-cost goods and services.

This issue, often raised by articulation theorists, is in need of further empirical investigation.

The present study argues that those researchers who explain the survival of small noncapitalist enterprises by the external relations they have with capitalist firms, at the expense of examining the internal dynamics of a small enterprise, are reductionist. The analysis of the internal aspects of production is indispensable for any understanding of what makes informal businesses viable and under what conditions they fail.

When agencies assisting refugees maintained control of the means of production and productive decisions, refugees felt alienated and unwilling to work hard. The failure of agencies to provide adequate machinery and training also affected the performance of small urban enterprises.

What is also important to understand is that, as Lanzetta and Murillo (1989, 109) put it, informality may be determined "primarily by survival needs of working-class households and, only secondarily, by the interest of large-scale firms." In their attempt to survive, small urban entrepreneurs employ certain strategies of survival – particular relations and organization of production – that make them more viable. They exploit the labour of apprentices, subcontractors, family members, friends, as well as their own, to cut the costs of production down. Although this exploitation is detrimental to small producers and those around them, it makes them competitive in the capitalist economy. Other organizational advantages of petty commodity production units are their adaptability to changes in demand and their merging of business affairs with those of the household.

These internal aspects of production – means, relationships, and organization – are more crucial for understanding how small urban enterprises work. Yet it should be recognized that these internal aspects are often responses to adverse conditions created by competition with the capitalist sector. The broad economic context in which petty commodity producers operate must also be considered. Not a single Salvadorean enterprise under study became capitalist in a strict sense, since capital was not separated from labour in any of them; every Salvadorean business owner participated in production.

In sum, to understand how small urban enterprises survive and succeed in the capitalist economy, it is necessary to link the analysis which focuses on internal aspects of production with that which outlines the constraints and pressures, and also the opportunities presented by the capitalist environment.

POLICY IMPLICATIONS

The examination of Salvadorean refugee enterprises draws attention to the importance of several policy issues. Some of them are relevant for the development of small urban enterprises in general, and some are more specifically related to the settlement of refugees.

SALVADOREAN ENTERPRISES AND
PROMOTION OF THE INFORMAL SECTOR

Students of the informal or petty commodity sector often ask whether relations between small urban producers and the capitalist sector are benign or exploitative (Moser 1978; Tokman 1978; Portes, Castells, and Benton 1989, 300–7). The answer has certain policy implications. If these relations are benign, they should be further promoted (Watanabe 1971; Bose 1974; House 1984). If, however, small urban enterprises are subordinated and exploited by capitalist firms, development programs for small urban enterprises should aim at making the small producers as independent of the capitalist sector as possible (Gerry 1979; Moser 1978; Schmitz 1982).

The present study examined various direct relations between small urban producers and capitalist enterprises. They included forward linkages (purchase of raw materials from capitalist enterprises), backward linkages (sale of goods or services to capitalist establishments), and subcontracting from capitalist firms. The analysis of forward linkages indicated that they made no impact on the economic performances of small producers. However, only those small Salvadorean producers who had good machinery and skills sold their goods or services to capitalist enterprises; their businesses could have been successful if they chose to sell to noncapitalist firms. As far as subcontracting is concerned, some producers chose to subcontract from capitalist enterprises because it was economically more profitable for them in comparison with other marketing possibilities. Other producers chose to subcontract because their machinery and skills were not good enough for them to procure other clients. In other words, their problem was not so much that they subcontracted but that their machinery and skills were insufficient. In sum, the conclusions drawn from the present research support the view that, for the development of small producers, it is not so important for whom they produce as whether they have a stable and growing clientele (Gerry 1979).

Another issue raised by certain students of the so-called informal sector concerns the feasibility of institutional assistance. Some writers, such as Moser (1978), Mosley (1978), and Bienefeld (1975), believe that, given strong competition from capitalist enterprises, institutional assistance to small producers hardly contributes to their economic development. Therefore, they argue, institutional assistance without corresponding sociopolitical structural reforms is useless.

The present study indicated that small Salvadorean producers did survive competition with capitalist enterprises. However, absence of adequate machinery, skills, and credit made it much more difficult for them to earn a viable income. It is precisely in this respect that institutions can assist small producers.

It should be remembered that Salvadorean refugee projects, unlike other small enterprises of the so-called informal sector, are not self-generating; they were created by institutions. The issue of institutional assistance is more important for their development than for that of other small urban enterprises. Yet it can be argued that aid in the form of better machinery, credit, or technical training can make the survival of any small producer easier, even if there is no corresponding sociopolitical reform.

Three policy issues relate to institutional assistance: first, the size of projects to be implemented through development schemes; second, the amount of aid to be offered per project; and, third, the impact of paternalistic treatment of project beneficiaries by agency workers.

Size of Projects

With reference to the size of refugee enterprises, Marmora argues in defence of medium- and large-scale refugee projects:

The larger size of the enterprise allows for the preparation of feasibility studies that narrow the margin of risk and give foresight as to the time factor in the return on the investment of capital. Such enterprises permit economy of scale that, in turn, facilitates greater productivity and, therefore, better quality competitive stand of the enterprise in the final products of these enterprises (which is harder for small firms), thus preventing competition with the receiving country and increasing that country's acquisition of foreign currency (Marmora 1986, 80).

Promotion of large-scale refugee projects would be in conflict with the philosophy behind the development of the informal sector – that large enterprises are capital but not labour intensive. Consequently, problems of unemployment of the refugee population would still exist and, instead of generating foreign currency, these enterprises would spend some of it on imported machinery. By contrast, small enterprises of the informal type allow considerably more labour to be employed at lower capital costs (see Harper 1985, for instance). Another argument that focuses on social relations among project managers can also be presented in defence of small refugee enterprises.

One of the problems encountered by Salvadorean refugee projects had to do with interpersonal conflicts among project members for either political reasons (a specific refugee phenomenon) or because they were given equal rights with reference to ownership and control of the means and process of production (see chapter 8). Individual or family projects were not affected by this problem, and, therefore, it seems more reasonable to implement them. Furthermore, as I have argued elsewhere (Basok, forthcoming), for cooperatives it is more difficult to maintain an informal structure that makes such small urban enterprises more viable.

If, for economic reasons, it is more advantageous to promote larger projects, a loan might be offered to only one member who has technical and business administration skills, while other members could be incorporated as wage-labourers or apprentices having certain wage and job-security guarantees by the owner. This strategy may create problems if everybody who has the required skills would prefer to be an owner, but people who are qualified to administer a collective project may not be numerous. Moreover, intentions of repatriation or third-country resettlement may discourage some refugees from assuming a debt if repayment is made a precondition for their exit visa. This arrangement would also solve another problem encountered in refugee projects – the withdrawal of some members from the projects for reasons of migration or repatriation. If all but one project beneficiary are incorporated as wage-labourers, they can easily be replaced by other refugees.

As Marmora (1986, 82) admits, both small- and large-scale refugee projects have failed in Costa Rica. At the same time, many small enterprises did survive. These projects survive if and when they are offered an adequate amount of aid.

Amount of Aid

In response to the high failure rate of the durable solution employment program and the swelling number of refugees in Costa Rica, a new employment program called local settlement was introduced. While the former gave relatively high grants to relatively few people, the latter made small grants possible to large numbers of refugees. Was the quality of the program sacrificed for the number of refugees benefiting from it?

It is difficult to talk about the quality of the durable solution program because of its high failure rate. However, as was argued earlier, the high failure and withdrawal rates were caused mainly by administrative mistakes, by the paternalistic attitude of agencies towards project members, and by interpersonal conflicts among project members. One would have hoped that by 1986 agencies in charge of refugee settlement would have learned from their mistakes, but that did not seem to be the case. The local settlement program advocates did not try to correct the problems faced by the durable solution projects. Instead, they promoted a reduction in the amount of aid. When incomes earned by project members and numbers of people employed in the program are related to the financial investment per project, the local settlement program demonstrated better results. In absolute terms, however, it produced little employment and relatively low incomes. Those refugees who generated relatively high incomes under this program were employed as contractors in construction. In other words, they were employed for wages, instead of creating their own businesses that would employ other refugees or the local labour force. These refugees, therefore, were in competition with national labour. Most developing countries that offer asylum to refugees try to avoid this situation.

It is difficult to suggest exactly the amount of assistance that should be offered to a refugee project. The amount will depend on the input requirements of individual enterprises. In general terms, the present study indicated there are three factors that affect income earned by petty commodity producers: quality of machinery, sufficiency of demand for goods or services, and adequacy of skills. First, small producers require machinery that will allow them to offer relatively good-quality goods or services relatively fast. Cheap machinery of the household type does not satisfy these requirements. At the same time, costly industrial machinery is expensive to maintain and does not correspond to the level of demand enjoyed by petty commodity producers. Immediate-level technology (semi-industrial machinery) is, therefore, most adequately suited for the needs of small producers.

Second, demand for goods or services offered by petty commodity producers depends partly on the quality of their machinery and on the location of the business (see chapter 6). Assistance with rent is required by those producers who cater to residents of their own neighbourhood and who need to be situated in an area that can give them steady demand and reasonable payoff. Demand also depends on competition from other small-scale producers or from capitalist enterprises. Market conditions must be carefully investigated before assisting a petty commodity producer.

Third, the experience of Salvadorean refugees in Costa Rica suggests that when refugees lack the skills necessary for their projects to work, their businesses do not succeed. Any agency promoting the development of such projects needs to offer some training.

Paternalism

Analysis of Salvadorean small enterprises in Costa Rica revealed that the paternalistic treatment of refugees involved in projects results in their lack of interest in staying in the project or in making it succeed. The paternalistic attitude possibly comes from a desire to do what is best for refugees, but the decision of what is best is taken one-sidedly, without any attempt to understand what refugees themselves think about it. Paternalism often comes spontaneously; agencies assisting refugees should make a conscious effort to control their ethnocentrism.

LOCAL SETTLEMENT VERSUS THIRD-COUNTRY RESETTLEMENT: A NEED FOR MORE RESEARCH

Next to voluntary repatriation, local settlement is considered to be the best solution for most refugees by UNHCR, developed countries' governments, and nongovernmental agencies assisting refugees. Yet while most refugees are encouraged to stay in the region, most research in the refugee field has been conducted in countries of resettlement – Canada, the United States, and Australia. Development aid to refugees in countries of first asylum has not been sufficiently analysed, and should be linked to theories of comparative development. This book offers the first step in this direction. It addresses questions of viability of small urban producers and the appropriateness of financing urban enterprises for refugees. Yet we need to remember that most refugees (especially those in Africa) are rural. More research needs to be conducted on the viability of rural projects, given constraints imposed by the world economic and political system.

Appendix

CALCULATION OF MONTHLY REPAYMENT OF DEBT

To calculate monthly repayment of an assumed loan from an agency, it was assumed that enterprise owners acquired a loan for three years at an annual interest rate of 6 per cent. This interest rate corresponds to the inflation rate of 0. It was also assumed that interest is paid off the balance. Monthly instalments were then calculated in the following way:

$$MI = \frac{I}{36} + \frac{K}{36}$$

$$K + I = \frac{K}{2}(1 + r)^t = \frac{K}{2}(1.06)^3 = 1.91\frac{K}{2}$$

$$I = 0.191\frac{K}{2} = 0.096\,K$$

$$MI = \frac{0.096\,K}{36} + \frac{K}{36} = 0.03\,K$$

where MI is monthly instalment, K is the cost of capital, I is interest, t is three years (since it was assumed that loans were given for three years), and r is an annual interest rate (6 per cent). Monthly repayment of the debt was then averaged for ten years (assumed duration of machinery) by multiplying MI by 0.3 (three years divided by ten).

Notes

PREFACE

1 In the African context, "durable solutions" include local settlement as well as repatriation and third-country resettlement. In Central America and Mexico, only local settlement is understood under the "durable solution" rubric.

2 Agencies working with refugees in Costa Rica equated "failure" with the closing down of the project either as a result of its being abandoned by project members or of its being shut down by an agency in charge. From the point of view of individual members placed in these projects, abandonment may not have been a "failure." In fact, these refugees abandoned the projects in order to move on to what they perceived as better economic occupations. From the point of view of a development agency, however, withdrawal from projects translated into failure, since the goal of the "durable solution" program was to make refugees self-sufficient by incorporating them into small enterprises. Grants were given to refugees to work in productive projects and to create more employment. (It is usually believed that small enterprises of this kind have good potential for generating employment). Funds were viewed as badly invested if these projects did not remain active.

3 See Blomstrom and Hettne (1984) and Eisenstadt (1973) for a discussion and criticism of the "modernization" paradigm.

CHAPTER TWO

1 The procedures for determining refugee status changed again when Nicaraguan refugees started fleeing to Costa Rica. To determine their status, the Costa Rican Refugee Office used a broader definition expressed in the 1984 Cartagena Declaration. What it meant in effect was that every Nicaraguan who applied for refugee status got it.

2 For a more detailed analysis of the differences in treatment of Nicaraguan and Salvadorean refugees by Costa Rican authorities see Basok 1990.

3 This perception changed at the end of the 1980s when the Costa Rican government representatives, NGO workers, Costa Rican union members, and the general public were all in agreement that the presence of Nicaraguan refugee in the country created a situation of potential economic crisis. *Tico Times*, 28 June 1989.

4 Oscar Arias, elected on 2 February 1986, was able to assume a more "neutral" and more independent position. During his term he normalized relations with Nicaragua, although he remained critical of the Sandinista government. He won a Nobel Prize for the peace plan he presented to presidents of the five Central American countries on 7 August 1987 in Guatemala City. In this plan, Arias appealed to Central American governments and the United States to stop aiding the contras.

CHAPTER THREE

1 The definition of the "informal" economy will be discussed in chapter 6. In Costa Rica, "informal" enterprises are equated with "microempresas" or small enterprises with no more than five workers.

2 In 1985, the victory of this party's candidate, Rafael Angel Calderon, was generally expected in the February 1986 election. In early 1986 public opinion suddenly swayed towards Oscar Arias, the presidential candidate of the centre right party, Liberación Nacional (National Liberation), who won the election.

CHAPTER FOUR

1 The exchange rate fluctuated in the 1980s between 50 and 75 colones to the U.S. dollar.

2 The cost of the basic food basket for a family of six was 2957 colones per month in 1982 in Costa Rica (MIDEPLAN 1983a, 17). According to the Central Bank data, prices went up 26 per cent between 1982 and 1983, thus increasing the cost of the basic food basket to 3373 colones per month by 1983.

3 Refugees often referred to OARS as *la casa de medicina* (the house of medicine) because of this service.

4 In February 1987, after I had left the field, twelve technical assistants working at DIGEPARE resigned. Reasons for their resignation were "administrative irregularities" within the institution. They claimed that the lack of intra- and inter-institutional coordination had meant that most of the activities programmed for the year 1986 had not been implemented. They also mentioned that projects that were approved for funding by DIGEPARE were not in fact profitable (*Universidad*, no. 776, March 1987).

5 The term "productive project" is translated from the Spanish *proyectos productivos*. It refers to projects that were production oriented, but also covers all projects that aimed to make refugees self-sufficient.

CHAPTER FIVE

1 DGATPIA (1984) reported the cost of employment in small enterprises created by it in Costa Rica to be 10,782 colones in 1980–2. In other words, this seems to be comparable with the LS program.

2 Calculations are based on information reported in interviews with project members. There are some discrepancies between these calculations, for instance, and information on investment reported by Carrizo (1985).

CHAPTER SIX

1 Emphasis on relations with the state is also found in a recent collection on the informal sector edited by Clark (1988).

2 LeBrun and Gerry (1975, 20) suggest that petty commodity production should be classified as a form rather than a mode of production. According to these writers, mode of production "refers essentially to the totality which is self-sufficient at both the super-structure level and at the economic base." "Forms" of production, in contrast, "exist at the margins of the capitalist mode of production but are nevertheless

integrated into and subordinate to it." According to Moser (1978, 1057), petty commodity production has never constituted a dominant mode of production but was articulated with feudalism or with capitalism.

CHAPTER SEVEN

1 "Capitalist enterprises" are defined in terms of size in this book. Those enterprises with more than ten workers are categorized as "capitalist." It would, of course, be more adequate to take into consideration participation of the enterprise owner in production or service delivery. However, this information was not available to the researcher. It can also be argued that a fewer-than-ten-person capitalist enterprise (where the owner is separated from the means of production) would in many economic aspects be similar to a noncapitalist one of the same size.
2 Owing to the deterioration of diplomatic and trade relations between Costa Rica and Nicaragua under the Monge administration (1982–6), Nicaraguan shoes were no longer imported to Costa Rica.

CHAPTER EIGHT

1 The notion of marginality has been under serious attack (see Lomnitz 1977, for instance). While poor people are linked into capitalist society through the consumption market and, at a more abstract level, are functional to accumulation within the capitalist sector (by serving as a reserve army of labour), their participation in the sphere of capitalist production is restricted. It is in this sense that one is justified in calling them (or at least those of them who are underemployed) marginal.

Bibliography

Alfred, Kathy. 1987. "Effects of u.s. and Canadian Policies on Latin American Refugees." *Refuge* 7, 1: 3–4

Ambos, Kai. 1987. "The Central American Refugee Crisis: A Comparative Study of the Refugee Situation and Refugee Policies of Costa Rica, Honduras and Nicaragua." Refugee Studies Programme, University of Oxford, mimeo

Arguello, Omar. 1981. "Estrategias de Supervivencia: un Concepto en Busca de su Contenido." *Demografía y Economía* 15, 2: 190–203

Basok, Tanya. 1990. "Welcome Some and Reject Others: Constraints and Interests Influencing Costa Rican Policies on Refugees," *International Migration Review* 24 (4): 722–47

– Forthcoming. "Individual, Household and Cooperative Production. The Case of Salvadorean Refugees in Costa Rica." *Canadian Journal of Latin American and Caribbean Studies*

Beneria, Lourdes. 1989. "Subcontracting and Employment Dynamics in Mexico City." In *The Informal Economy: Studies in Advanced and Less Developed Countries*, edited by Alejandro Portes, Manuel Castells, and Lauren A. Benton. Baltimore and London: The Johns Hopkins University Press

Bernstein, Henry. 1988. "Capitalism and Petty-Bourgeois Production: Class Relations and Divisions of Labour." *Journal of Peasant Studies* 15, 2: 258–71

Bettelheim, C. 1972. "Theoretical Comments." In *Unequal Exchange*, by A. Emmanuel. New York: Monthly Review Press. Appendix 1

Betts, T.F. 1984. "Evolution and Promotion of the Integrated Rural Development Approach to Refugee Policy in Africa." *Africa Today* 31: 7–24

Bienefeld, Manfred. 1975. "The Informal Sector and Peripheral Capitalism: The Case of Tanzania." *International Development Studies (IDS) Bulletin* 6, 3: 53–73

Blachman, Morris J., and Ronald G. Hellman. 1986. "Costa Rica." In *Confronting Revolution: Security through Diplomacy in Central America,* edited by Morris J. Blachman et al. New York: Pantheon Books

Blincow, Malcolm. 1986. "Scavengers and Recycling: A Neglected Domain of Production." *Labour Capital and Society* 19, 1: 94–116

Blomstrom, Magnus, and Bjorn Hettne. 1984. *Development Theory in Transition. The Dependency Debate and Beyond: Third World Responses.* London: Zed Books

Bollinger, William, and Daniel Manny Lund. 1982. "Minority Oppression: Toward Analyses That Clarify and Strategies That Liberate." *Latin American Perspectives* 9, 2: 2–27

Booth, David. 1975. "Andre Gunder Frank: An Introduction and Appreciation." In *Beyond the Sociology of Development,* edited by Ivar Oxaal, Tony Barnett, and David Booth. London: Routledge and Kegan Paul

Bose, A.N. 1974. *The Informal Sector in the Calcutta Metropolitan Economy.* Geneva: ILO World Employment Programme, Working Paper 4

Bradby, Barbara. 1975. "The Destruction of Natural Economy." *Economy and Society* 4, 2: 127–61

Breton, Raymond. 1964. "Institutional Completeness of Ethnic Communities and Personal Relations of Immigrants." *American Journal of Sociology* 70: 193–205

– 1978. "Stratification and Conflict between Ethnolinguistic Communities with Different Social Structures." *Canadian Review of Sociology and Anthropology* 15, 2: 148–57

Bromley, Ray. 1985. "Introduction." In *Planning for Small Enterprises in Third World Cities,* edited by R. Bromley. Oxford, New York: Pergamon Press

Browning, David. 1971. *El Salvador: Landscape and Society.* Oxford: Clarendon Press

Buechler, Hans. 1982. "Small Traders Do Better in Bolivia." *Geographical Magazine* 54: 518–19

Burke, Melvin. 1976. "El Systema de Plantación y la Proletarización del Trabajo Agrícola en El Salvador." *Estudios Centroamericanos* 31, 335–6: 473–86

Camarda, Renato. 1985. *Forced to Move: Salvadorean Refugees in Honduras*. San Francisco: Solidarity Publications

Campos, Nidia. 1985. "Desfase entre la Formulación y la Aplicación de las Políticas en Materia Laboral del Refugiado en Costa Rica." San José: School of Social Work, Faculty of Social Sciences, University of Costa Rica. Mimeo

Cardoso, F.H. 1972. "Dependency and Development in Latin America." *New Left Review* 74: 83–95

Carrizo, Amanda. 1985. "Diagnóstico y Evaluación de los Proyectos de Refugiados Ejecutados por la Agencia Cáritas." San José: ILO-UNHCR. December. Mimeo.

– 1986. "La Unidad de Soluciones Durables: Una Experiencia de Sistematización e Integración de Refugiados Urbanos." San José: ILO-UNHCR. Mimeo

Castells, Manuel, and Alejandro Portes. 1989. "World Underneath: The Origins, Dynamics, and Effects of the Informal Economy." In *The Informal Economy: Studies in Advanced and Less Developed Countries*, edited by Alejandro Portes, Manuel Castells, and Lauren A. Benton. Baltimore and London: The Johns Hopkins University Press

Chambers, Robert. 1979. "Rural Refugees in Africa: What the Eye Does Not See." *Disasters* 3: 381–92

Chapin, Mac. 1989. "The 500,000 Invisible Indians of El Salvador." *Cultural Survival Quarterly* 13, 3: 11–16

Charmes, Jacques. 1980. "Les Contradictions de Développement du Secteur Non Structuré." *Revue Tiers-Monde* 21, 82: 321–35

Chevalier, Jacques. 1982. "There Is Nothing Simple about Simple Commodity Production." *Journal of Peasant Studies* 10, 4: 153–86

Clark, Gracia, ed. 1988. *Traders versus the State: Anthropological Approaches to Unofficial Economies*. Boulder and London: Westview Press

Clark, Lance. 1986. "Dependency Syndrome: Another Look." *Refugees Magazine* 29 (May): 35–6

Clay, Jason, and Bonnie Holcombe. 1985. *Politics and the Ethiopian Famine, 1984–85*. Cambridge, Mass: Cultural Survival. December

Colindres, Eduardo. 1976. "La Tenencia de la Tierra en El Salvador." *Estudios Centoamericanos* 31, 335–6: 463–72

CONAPARE. 1983a. "Plan Global de Criterios Para Proyectos de Solución Durable Para Refugiados y Nacionales." San José, Costa Rica. Mimeo

– 1983b. "Situación de los Proyectos Para Refugiados en Costa Rica." San José, Costa Rica. Mimeo

Cuenod, Jacques. 1989. "Refugees: Develoment or Relief?" In *Refugees and International Relations*, edited by Gil Loescher and Laila Monahan. Oxford: Oxford University Press

Davies, Rob. 1979. "Informal Sector or Subordinate Mode of Production? A Model." In *Casual Work and Poverty in Third World Cities*, edited by Ray Bromley and Chris Gerry. Chichester, Eng., and New York: Wiley

Dewar, D., and V. Watson. 1982. "Urbanization, Unemployment and Petty Commodity Production and Trading: Comparative Cases in Cape Town." In *Living Under Apartheid*, edited by David M. Smith. London: George Allen and Unwin

DGATPIA. 1984. "Importancia de la Pequeña Industria en la Economía Nacional." Ministerio de Industria, Energía y Minas, Dirección General de Pequeña Industria y Artesanía, San José, Costa Rica. Mimeo

Díaz-Polanco, Héctor. 1982. "Indigenismo, Populism, and Marxism." *Latin American Perspectives* 9, 2: 42–61

Dos Santos, T. 1970. "The Structure of Dependence." *American Economic Review* 60: 231–6

Dowty, Alan. 1987. *Closed Borders: The Contemporary Assault on Freedom of Movement*. New Haven and London: Yale University Press

Dumont, René, with Marcel Mazoyer. 1969. *Socialism and Development*. New York, Washington: Praeger Press

Duque, J., and E. Pastrana. 1973. "Las Estrategias de Supervivencia Económica de las Unidades Familiares del Sector Popular Urbano: Una Investigación Exploratoria." Programa ELAS/CELADE, Santiago, Chile. Mimeo

Durham, William H. 1979. *Scarcity and Survival in Central America*. Stanford: Stanford University Press

Eisenstadt, S.N. 1973. *Tradition, Change and Modernity*. New York: Wiley

"Estudio Sobre la Situación Jurídica de Asilados, Refugiados y Personas Desplazada." 1983. San José. Mimeo

Evaluación Económica de las Reformas, 1982. Instituto de Investigaciones Económicas, Estudios Centroamericanos, Vol. 37, nos. 403–404

Fagen, Richard R. 1987. *Forging Peace: The Challenge of Central America*. New York: B. Blackwell

Ferris, Elizabeth G. 1987. *The Central American Refugees*. New York: Praeger Publishers

Frank, Andre Gunder. 1970. "The Development of Underdevelopment." In *Imperialism and Underdevelopment*, edited by Robert I. Rhodes. New York: Monthly Review

Friedmann, Harriet. 1980. "Household Production and the National Economy: Concepts for the Analysis of Agrarian Formations." *Journal of Peasant Studies* 7, 2: 158–84

– 1986. "Postscript: Petty Commodity Production." *Labour Capital and Society* 19, 1: 117–26

Furtado, Celso. 1971. *Development and Underdevelopment*. Berkley: University of California Press

Gerry, Chris. 1978. "Underemployment: Petty Production and Government Promotion Schemes in Senegal." *International Development Studies Bulletin* 19, 3: 11–16

– 1979. "Small-scale Manufacturing and Repairs in Dakar: A Survey of Market Relations within the Urban Economy." In *Casual Work and Poverty in Third World Cities*, edited by Ray Bromley and Chris Gerry. Chichester, England, and New York: Wiley

Gershuny, J.I. 1979 "The Informal Economy: Its Role in Post-Industrial Society." *Futures* 11, 1: 3–15

Ghose, Ajit Kumar. 1983. *Agrarian Reform in Contemporary Development Countries*. London and Canberra: Croom Helm; New York: St Martin's Press

Goodman, David, and Michael Redclift. 1981. *From Peasant to Proletarian: Capitalist Development and Agrarian Transitions*. Oxford: Basil Blackwell

– 1985. "Capitalism, Petty Commodity Production and the Farm Enterprise." *Sociologia Ruralis* 25, 3/4: 230–47

Haans, Han. 1985. "El Sector Informal en Centroamérica." ILO PREALC. Mimeo

Harper, Malcolm. 1985. "Why Should We Try to Help Small Enterprises?" In *Planning for Small Enterprises in Developing Countries: Case Studies and Conclusions*. London: Intermediate Technology Publications

Harrell-Bond, B.E. 1986. *Imposing Aid: Emergency Assistance to Refugees*. Oxford: Oxford University Press

Harriss, Barbara. 1978. "Quasi-Formal Employment Structures and Behaviour in the Unorganized Urban Economy, and the Reverse: Some Evidence from South India." *World Development* 6, 9/10: 1077–86

Hart, Keith. 1970. "Small Scale Entrepreneurs in Ghana and Development Planning." *Journal of Development Studies* 6, 4: 104–20

– 1973. "Informal Income Opportunities and Urban Employment in Ghana." *Journal of Modern African Studies* 11, 1: 61–89

House, William J. 1984. "Nairobi's Informal Sector: Dynamic Entrepreneurs or Surplus Labour?" *Economic Development and Change* 32, 2: 276–302

ICIHI (Independent Commission on International Humanitarian Rights).
1986. *Refugees: Dynamic of Displacement*. London: Zed Books

ILO (International Labour Office). 1972. ILO *Report on Employment, Incomes and Equality in Kenya*. Geneva: ILO

Inter-Religious Task Force on Central America and Central American Concern. 1986. *Central American Refugee: Hoping for Peace*

Jimenez, Virginia. 1985. "Analisis del Trabajo Realizado en el Programa de Refugiados por Cáritas de Costa Rica. Período Octubre 1981–Julio 1985." San José, Costa Rica: CONAPARE. Mimeo

Kahn, Joel. 1986. "Problems in the Analysis of Peasant Ideology." *Labour Capital and Society* 19, 1: 36–69

Keely, Charles. 1981. *Global Refugee Policy: The Case for a Development-Oriented Strategy*. New York: Population Council

Kennedy, P. 1981. "The Role and Position of Petty Producers in a West African City." *Journal of Modern African Studies* 19, 4: 565–94

Kent, Randolph. 1987. *The Anatomy of the Disaster Relief: The International Network in Action*. London: Frances Pinter

Laclau, Ernesto. 1971. "Feudalism and Capitalism in Latin America." *New Left Review* 67: 19–38

Langdon, S. 1975. "Multinational Corporations, Taste Transfer and Underdevelopment: A Case Study from Kenya." *Review of African Political Economy* 2: 12–35

Lanzetta de Pardo, Mónica, and Gabriel Murillo Castaño, with Alvaro Triana Soto. 1989. "Informal Sector versus Informalized Labor Relations in Uruguay." In *The Informal Economy: Studies in Advanced and Less Developed Countries*, edited by Alejandro Portes, Manuel Castells, and Lauren A. Benton. Baltimore and London: Johns Hopkins University Press

Lappe, Frances Moore, and Joseph Collins. 1986. *World Hunger: Twelve Myths*. New York: Grove Press

LeBrun, Oliver, and Chris Gerry. 1975. "Petty Producers and Capitalism." *Review of African Political Economy* 3: 20–32

Lem, Winnie. 1988. "Household Production and Reproduction in Rural Languedoc: Social Relations of Petty Commodity Production in Murviel-Les-Beziers." *Journal of Peasant Studies* 15, 4: 500–29

Leonard, M. Willey. 1980. "Quelques réflexions sur l'expérience de Madagascar en matière de politique artisanale." *Revue Tiers-Monde* 21, 82: 337–51

Lipton, Michael. 1977. *Why Poor People Stay Poor: Urban Bias in World Development*. London: Temple Smith

Loescher, Gil. 1988. "Humanitarianism and Politics in Central America." *Political Science Quarterly* 103, 2: 295–320

Lomnitz, Larrissa Adler. 1977. *Networks and Marginality: Life in a Mexican Shantytown*. New York: Academic Press

Long, Norman, and Paul Richardson. 1978. "Informal Sector, Petty Commodity Production, and the Social Relations of Small-Scale Enterprise." In *The New Economic Anthropology*, edited by John Clammer. London: Macmillan

MacEwan Scott, Alison. 1979. "Who Are the Self-Employed?" In *Casual Work and Poverty in Third World Cities*, edited by Ray Bromley and Chris Gerry. Chichester, Eng., and New York: Wiley

Marmora, Lelio. 1984. "Migraciones Laborales e Integración del Refugiado en Costa Rica." Buenos Aires: ILO-UNHRC. Mimeo

– 1986. "Durable Solutions for Central American Refugees." In *Proceedings of the Inter-American Conference on Migration Trends and Policies*, edited by Mary Ann Larkin. Washington: Centre for Immigration Policy and Refugee Assistance, Georgetown University

Marx, Karl. 1962. *Capital*, vol, II. Moscow: Foreign Language Publishing House

– 1964. *The Economic and Philosophical Manuscripts of 1844*. New York: International Publishers

– 1970. *Capital*, vol. II. London: Lawrence and Wishart

Mason, Linda, and Roger Brown. 1983. *Rice, Rivalry, and Politics: Managing Cambodian Relief*. Notre Dame and London: University of Notre Dame Press

McGee, Terence. 1979. "Conservation and Dissolution in the Third World City. The 'Shanty-Town' as an Element of Conservation." *Development and Change* 10, 1: 1–22

McGee, T.G. 1974. *Hawkers in Hong Kong: A Study of Planning and Policy in a Third World City*. Centre of Asian Studies, University of Hong Kong

Meillassoux, Claude. 1972. "From Reproduction to Production. A Marxist Approach to Economic Anthropology." *Economy and Society* 1, 1: 93–105

– 1981. *Maidens, Meals and Money*. Cambridge: Cambridge University Press

MIDEPLAN. 1983a. "El Deterioro de la Condición Social de los Costarricenses." San José, Costa Rica: Ministerio de Planificación Nacional y Política Económica. Mimeo

– 1983b. *Costa Rica: El Empleo en la Crisis Actual, 1980–1982*. San José, Costa Rica: Ministerio de Planificación Nacional y Política Económica,

División de Planificación y Coordinación Sectorial, Departamento de Población. Mimeo

- 1984. "La Crisis y la Evolución del Empleo y Los Ingresos en Costa Rica." San José, Costa Rica: Ministerio de Planificación Nacional y Política Económica. Mimeo

- 1985. "La Situación del Refugiado en Costa Rica." San José, Costa Rica: Ministerio de Planificación Nacional y Política Económica. Mimeo

Ministerio de Trabajo y Seguro Social. 1983. "Algunas Características del Sector Informal Urbano en Costa Rica." San José, Costa Rica: Dirección General de Planificación del Trabajo y Empleo, Subdirección de Políticas y Planes. Mimeo

Ministerio de Trabajo y Seguro Social. 1986. "Programas de Empleo de Emergencia: La Experiencia del Ministerio de Trabajo y Seguridad Social." In *Mas Allá de la Crisis*, edited by PREALC, ILO. Mimeo

Miras, Claude de. 1980. "Le Secteur de Subsistance dans les Branches de Production a Abidjan." *Revue Tiers-Monde* 21, 82: 353–71

Moller, Allois. 1985a. "La Pequeña Industria y Artesanía en Costa Rica. Diagnóstico Institucional y Propuesta de Programa de Fomento." San José, Costa Rica: MIDEPLAN. Mimeo

— 1985b. "Segmentación del Mercado en el Area Metropolitana de San José." San José, Costa Rica: MIDEPLAN. Mimeo

Montes, Segundo. 1986. *El Salvador 1986: En Busca de Soluciónes para los Desplazados*. Instituto de Investigaciones e Instituto de Derechos Humanos de la Universidad Centroamericana de El Salvador "José Simeon Cañas" (UCA)

Montgomery, Tommie Sue. 1982. *Revolution in El Salvador: Origins and Evolution*. Boulder, Colorado: Westview Press

Moody, Roger, ed. 1988. *The Indigenous Voices: Visions and Realities*. London: Zed Books

Moser, Caroline. 1977. "The Dual Economy and Marginality Debate and the Contribution of Micro Analysis: Market Sellers in Bogota." *Development and Change* 8: 465–89

- 1978. "Informal Sector or Petty Commodity Production: Dualism or Development in Urban Development?" *World Development* 6, 9/10: 1041–64

Mosley, Paul. 1978. "Implicit Models and Policy Recommendations: Policy Towards the 'Informal Sector' in Kenya." *International Development Studies Bulletin* 9, 3: 3–10

North, Lisa. 1985. *Bitter Grounds: Roots of Revolt in El Salvador*. Third edition. Toronto: Between the Lines

O'Brien, Phillip. 1975. "A Critique of Latin American Theories of Dependency." In *Beyond the Sociology of Development*, edited by Ivar Oxaal, Tony Barnett, and David Booth. London: Routledge and Kegan Paul

OFIPLAN. 1981. "Población, Fuerza de Trabajo y Empleo en Costa Rica, Estudio Descriptivo del Período 1973–1980." San José, Costa Rica: Oficina de Planificación Nacional y Política Económica, División de Planificación y Coordinación Sectorial, Departamento de Población. Mimeo

Ortiz, Roxanne Dunbar. 1984. *Indians of the Americas: Human Rights and Self-Determination*. London: Zed Books

Out of Ashes: The Lives and Hopes of Refugees from El Salvador and Guatemala. 1985. London: El Salvador Committee for Human Rights, Guatemala Committee for Human Rights, War on Want Campaigns Ltd

Peattie, Lisa R. 1980. "Anthropological Perspectives on the Concepts of Dualism, the Informal Sector and Marginality in Developing Urban Economies." *International Regional Science Review* 5, 1: 1–31

– 1982. "What Is Done with the 'Informal Sector'? A Case Study of Shoe Manufacturers in Colombia." In *Towards a Political Economy of Urbanization in Third World Countries*, edited by Helen I. Safa. Delhi: Oxford University Press

PISPAL. 1978. *Líneas Prioritarias de Investigación para el III Fase*. Mexico

Portes, A. 1978. "The Informal Sector and the World Economy." *International Development Studies Bulletin* 9, 4: 35–40

Portes, Alejandro, and John Walton. 1981. *Labour, Class and the International System*. New York: Academic Press

Portes, Alejandro, Manuel Castells, and Lauren A. Benton, eds. 1989. *The Informal Economy: Studies in Advanced and Less Developed Countries*. Baltimore and London: Johns Hopkins University Press

PREALC. 1984. *Costa Rica: Características de las Microempresas y sus Dueños*. ILO

– 1985. *Household Behaviour Economic Crisis. Costa Rica 1979–1982*. Working Document, ILO

– 1986. *Cambio y Polarización Ocupacional en Centroamerica*. ILO

Report on Human Rights in El Salvador. 1983. Americas Watch Committee and the American Civil Liberties Union, Second Supplement. Centre for National Security. Washington, DC

Richmond, Anthony. 1988. "Sociological Theories of International Migration: The Case of Refugees." *Current Sociology* 36, 2: 7–25

Roberts, Bryan R. 1989. "Employment Structure, Life Cycle, and Life Chances: Formal and Informal Sectors in Guadalajara." In *The Informal*

Economy: Studies in Advanced and Less Developed Countries, edited by Alejandro Portes, Manuel Castells, and Lauren Benton. Baltimore and London: Johns Hopkins University Press

Rodriguez, Daniel. 1981. "Discusiones en Torno al Concepto de Estrategias de Supervivencia. Relatoría del Taller sobre Estrategias de Supervivencia." *Demografía y Economía* 15, 2 (46): 238–52

Rogge, John R. 1987. "When Is Self-Sufficiency Achieved? The Case of Rural Africa." In *Refugees: A Third World Dilemma*, edited by John R. Rogge. New Jersey: Rowman and Littlefield

Rojas, Manuel B. 1984. "Costa Rica: El Final de Una Era." In *La Crisis Centroamericana*, edited by Daniel Camacho and Manuel B. Rojas. San José: Editorial Universitaria Centroamericana, FLACSO

Rovira, Jorge. 1985. "El Desarrollo de Costa Rica y Su Crisis en el Período de Postguerra: 1948–1984." *Annuario de Estudios Centroamericanos* 11, 1

Schmitz, Hubert. 1982. *Manufacturing in the Backyard*. London: Frances Printer

Senghaas-Knobloch, Eva. 1977. "Informal Sector and Peripheral Capitalism: A Critique of Prevailing Concepts of Development." *Manpower and Unemployment Research* 10, 2: 3–24

Shawcross, William. 1984. *Quality of Mercy*. New York: Simon and Schuster

Simon, Laurence, and James C. Stephens Jr. 1981. "Reforma Agraria en El Salvador (1980–1981): Su Impacto en la Sociedad Salvadoreña." *Estudios Centroamericanos* 36, 389: 173–80

Smart, Josephine. 1988. "How to Survive in Illegal Hawking in Hong Kong." In *Traders Versus the State: Anthropological Approaches to Unofficial Economies*, edited by Gracia Clark. Boulder and London: Westview Press

Smith, Carol. 1984. "Does a Commodity Economy Enrich the Few while Ruining the Masses? Differentiation among Petty Commodity Producers in Guatemala." *Journal of Peasant Studies* 11, 3: 60–95

Souza, Paolo, and Victor E. Tokman. 1976. "The Informal Urban Sector in Latin America." *International Labour Review* 114, 3: 355–65

Standing, Guy. 1977. "Urban Workers and Patterns of Employment." In *Studies in Urban Labour Market Behaviour*, edited by Subbiah Kannappan. Geneva: ILO

Stein, Barry N. 1987. "ICARA II: Burden Sharing and Durable Solutions." In *Refugees: A Third World Dilemma*, edited by John R. Rogge. New Jersey: Rowman and Littlefield

Tangri, Shanti S. 1982. "Family Structure and Industrial Entrepreneurship in Urban India: The Evolution of a Field Study." In *Towards a Political Economy of Urbanization in Third World Countries*, edited by Helen I. Safa. Delhi: Oxford University Press

Tokman, Victor. 1978. "An Exploration into the Nature of Informal-Formal Sector Relationship." *World Development* 6, 9/10: 1065–75

Torrado, Susan. 1981. "Sobre los Conceptos de 'Estrategias Familiares de Vida' y 'Proceso de Reproducción de la Fuerza de Trabajo': Notas Teoricometodológicas." *Demografía y Economía* 15, 2 (46): 204–33

University for Peace. 1985. "Los Refugiados Centroamericanos." Costa Rica. Mimeo

Valdes, Ximena, and Miguel Acuña. 1981. "Precisiones Metodológicas Sobre las Estrategias de Supervivencia." *Demografía y Economía* 15, 2 (46): 234–7

Van Dijk, Meine Pieter. 1980. "La Réussite des Petits Entrepreneurs dans le Secteur Informel de Ouagadougou (Haute-Volta)." *Revue Tiers-Monde* 21, 84: 373–403

Vega, Jose Luis. 1984. "Central American Refugees in Costa Rica." San José: Hemisphere Migration Project. Mimeo

– 1986. *Hacía una Interpretación del Desarrollo Costarriense: Ensayo Sociológico*. Fifth Edition. San José: Editorial Porvenir S.A., Colección Debate

Wallerstein, Immanuel. 1977. "Rural Economy in Modern World Society." *Studies in Comparative International Development* 12, 1: 29–40

Watanabe, S. 1971. "Subcontracting Industrialization and Employment Creation." *International Labour Review* 104, 1: 51–76

Weiner, Myron. 1985. "On International Migration and International Relations." *Population and Development Review* 11, 3: 441–55

Wellings, Paul, and Michael Sutcliffe. 1984. "Developing the Urban Informal Sector in South Africa: The Reformist Paradigm and its Fallacies." *Development and Change* 15, 4: 517–50

Wolpe, Harold. 1972. "Capitalism and Cheap Labour-Power in South Africa: From Segregation to Apartheid." *Economy and Society* 1, 4: 425–57

World Refugee Survey: 1988 in Review. U.S. Committee for Refugees, American Council for Nationalities Service. Washington, DC

Ybarra, Josep-Antoni. 1989. "Informalization in the Valencian Economy: A Model for Underdevelopment." In *The Informal Economy: Studies in Advanced and Less Developed Countries*, edited by Alejandro Portes,

Manuel Castells, and Lauren A. Benton. Baltimore and London: Johns Hopkins University Press

Zarjevski, Yefime. 1988. *A Future Preserved: International Assistance to Refugees*. Oxford: Pergamon Press

Zolberg, Aristide R., Astri Suhrke, and Sergio Aguayo. 1986. "International Factors in the Formation of Refugee Movement." *International Migration Review* 20, 2: 151–69

– 1989. *Escape from Violence: Conflict and the Refugee Crisis in Developing World*. New York, Oxford: Oxford University Press

Index